New Missal Same Mass

*Understanding the English Translation of
the New Roman Missal*

New Missal Same Mass

*Understanding the English Translation of
the New Roman Missal*

by

Rev. Fr. S. Joseph Lionel

Asian Trading Corporation
Bangalore, India
2010

Imprimatur: + Bernard Moras, Archbishop of Bangalore, India.
December 8, 2010

Rev.Fr. S. Joseph Lionel, St.Peter's Pontifical Seminary, 61, 8th Main, Malleswaram west P.O. Bangalore 560055, Karnataka, INDIA

e-mail: jlionel@gmail.com

First Edition: 1000 copies
Second Edition: 2000 copies
Price: Rs. 75.00/-

Foreign: US $ 10

Printing : Deccan Data Forms
44, 18th Cross, Bagalagunte
Bangalore - 560 073.
Ph: 080-23721533

ISBN : 81-7086-591-3

Published by : Asian Trading Corporation
58, 2nd Cross, Da Costa Layout, St. Mary's Town,
Bangalore - 560 084.
Tel : (080) 2548 7444, 2549 0444 Fax : (080) 2547 9444
E-mail : atcbooks@gmail.com Website : www.atcbooks.in

THE ARCHDIOCESE OF BOMBAY

His Eminence Oswald Cardinal Gracias
Archbishop of Bombay

Archbishop's House
Mumbai
India

Foreword

Beginning from the First Sunday of Advent, that is 27 November 2011, the words we say and hear at the Holy Mass are going to change with the introduction of the recently approved English translation of the *editiotypicatertia* of the *MissaleRomanum* published in 2002. This is an unique opportunity to catechize our Catholic faithful about the deeper meaning of the Sacrament of the Eucharist and to explain the rich meaning of the liturgical texts, so that it may bring an authentic liturgical renewal in the Church. Our faithful in the English speaking countries and their pastors are indeed looking for resources to offer them a proper understanding of the Missal and for catechetical aids to help them prepare for receiving the new Missal. Realizing the urgency of the situation and the opportunity to catechize, Rev. Fr. S. Joseph Lionel, Professor of Liturgy at St. Peter's Pontifical Seminary, Bangalore, India is bringing out this book titled, "New Missal...Same Mass: Understanding the Translation of the New Roman Missal 2002", which I am confident hope that the Catholics both in India and other English speaking countries will find useful.

In his book, Fr. Lionel explains how the new translation seeks to reclaim the richness of the original texts. In the liturgical tradition the words of the Missal often echo passages from the Bible. The new translation will bring such biblical allusions to prominence and better connect the prayers in the Missal to the Lectionary. As our Holy Father Pope Benedict XVI says in his recent Post-Synodal Apostolic Exhortation, *Verbum Domini*, "Every liturgical action is by its very nature steeped in Sacred Scripture" (#52). In this book, the author seeks to highlight such richness in the prayers of the

Roman Missal in their historical and theological contexts. Such explanation provides solid foundation for liturgical catechesis, a much needed effort in every diocese.

The book is well researched within a language that avoids an excessive use of technical words. Pastors, members of Liturgical Commissions, students of liturgy and our lay faithful will find much material to help them enter more deeply into the mystery of the Eucharist.

Therefore, while appreciating and thanking Fr. Lionel for his strenuous work in authoring this book, I wish that English speaking Catholics may have easy access to this book and benefit by its content. May God bless his work and bring it to fruition in the liturgical renewal much desired by the Second Vatican Council.

His Eminence Oswald Cardinal Gracias
Archbishop of Bombay
President of CBCI, India
Vice-Chairman, *Vox Clara Committee*, Rome

Contents

viii

Abbreviations

AAS   Acta Apostolicæ Sedis. The official bulletin of the Holy See. Before 1908 the title was Acta Sanctæ Sedis.

Abbott   W. M. Abbott. ed. *The Documents of Vatican II*. New York: Herder and Herder, 1966. English translation of the council documents indicated "Abbott" is taken from this edition.

ACW   *Ancient Christian Writers*. Westminster, MD.: The Newman Press, 1967.

ANCL   *Anti-Nicene Christian Library: Translations of the Writings of the Fathers*. eds. A. Roberts and J. Donaldson. Edinburgh: T and T Clark, 1869ff.

Bugnini   Bugnini, A. *The Reform of the Liturgy 1948-1975*. Translated by. M. J. O'Connell. Collegeville, MN.: The Liturgical Press, 1983 unless his other titles are specifically mentioned in the footnotes.

CCSL   *Corpus Christianorum,* Series Latina.

CDW   Congregation for Divine Worship.

CDWDS   Congregation for Divine Worship and Discipline of the Sacraments. On 11 July 1975 CDW became CDWDS.

CIEL   Centre International d'études Liturgiques.

CICSL   The Consilium for the Implementation of the Constitution of the Sacred Liturgy.

Cor.Pr   Moeller, E. *Corpus Præfationum*. vol.161A, IX-X. *Corpus Christianorum Series Latina* 161. Turnholti: Brepols, 1981.

Cor.Or   Moeller, E. *Corpus Orationum*. vol. 1 ff. *Corpus Christianorum Series Latina* 160. Turnholti: Brepols, 1991.

CSEL   Corpus Scriptorum Ecclesiasticorum Latinorum.

Consilium   Consilium ad exsequendam Constitutionem de Sacra Liturgia. Commission for the implementation of the Constitution on the liturgy by Paul VI Motu Proprio, "Sacram Liturgiam." 25 January 1964 in AAS 56 (1964): 139-144.

Con.MR   *Concordantia et Indices Missalis Romani.* Presentazione di S.E. Mons. Francesco Pio Tamburrino. Citta del vaticana: Libreria Editrice Vaticana, 2002.

CSR   Congregation of Sacred Rites. Constituted by Sixtus V in 1588. In 1969 it was divided into two congregations, one for the causes of the saints and one for the Divine Worship (CDW) by Paul VI's Apostolic Constitution, "Sacra Ritum Congregatio." AAS 61 (1969): 297-305. In the same year, the Consilium was integrated into CDW.

DOL   *Documents on the Liturgy 1963-1979: Conciliar, Papal and Curial Texts.* Collegeville, M.N.: The Liturgical Press, 1982.

DV   *Dei Verbum,* Second Vatican Council's Dogmatic Constitution on Divine Revelation, November 18, 1965.

EL   *Ephemerides Liturgicæ,* Rome.

EN   *Evangelii Nuntiandi,* post-synodal apostolic exhortation of Pope John Paul II on Evangelization of the Modern world, December 8, 1975.

EO   *Ecclesia Orans,* San Anselmo, Rome.

Flannery   Flannery, A. ed. *Vatican Council II: The Conciliar and Post Conciliar Documents.* New York: Costello Publishing Company, 1996.

GIRM   General Instruction to the Roman Missal. The 5th edition.

ICEL   The International Commission on English in the Liturgy. The constitution of ICEL is published in *Notitiæ* 108-109 (1975): 245-248. See also *Notitiæ* 11 (1965): 339-345.

IGMR   *Institutio Generalis Missalis Romani* in *Missale Romanum: editio typica tertia.* Typis Vaticanis, 2002.

GS   *Gaudium et Spes,* Second Vatican Council's Pastoral Constitution on the Church in the Modern World, December 7, 1965.

LDS   Liturgy Documentary Series 2. Washington D.C.: United States Conference of Catholic Bishops, 2003.

LG   *Lumen Gentium*, Second Vatican Council's Dogmatic Constitution on the Church

Liturgiam Authenticam: Congregation for Divine Worship and Discipline of Sacraments, *Liturgiam Authenticam: Fifth instruction on Vernacular Translation of the Roman Liturgy.* Washington, DC: USCCB, 2001.

LMD   *La Maison-Dieu*

LQF   Liturgiewissenschaftliche Quellen und Forschungen – Instituts der Abtei Maria Laach.

MP 1738   *Missale Parisiense 1738.* Parisiis: Sumptibus bibliopolarum ufuum parifienfium, 1738.

MP 1739   *Missale Parisiense 1739.* Parisiis: Sumptibus bibliopolarum ufuum parifienfium, 1739.

MR 1570   Missale Romanum of Pius V promulgated by "Quo primum" in 1570 *Missale Romanum (1570): Editio Princeps.* Libreria Editrice Vaticana, 1998.

MR 1962   *Missale Romanum (1962).* Libreria Editrice Vaticana, 2007.

MR 1970   *Missale Romanum: Editio Typica.* Libreria Editrice Vaticana, 1970.

MR 1975   *Missale Romanum: Editio Typica Altera.* Libreria Editrice Vaticana, 1975.

MR 2002   *Missale Romanum: Editio Typica Tertia.* Libreria Editrice Vaticana, 2002.

Not   *Notitiæ*, official bulletin of the Sacred Congregation for Divine Worship.

NJBC   Brown, R. E., J. A. Fitzmyer, and R. E. Murphy. eds. *The New Jerome Biblical Commentary.* London: Prentice Hall Inc., 1990.

NRT   *Nouvelle Revue Théologique*

PG   Patrologia Græca. 161 vols. 1857-1865.

PL   Patrologia Latina. 217 vols. 1878-1890.

QL   *Questions Liturgicæ*

RBén   *Révue Bénédictine*

RL   *Rivista liturgica*

S.Comp   Ward, A. and C. Johnson. *The Prefaces of the Roman Missal: A Source Compendium with Concordance and Indices.* Rome: Congregation for Divine Worship, 1989.

S.Chr   *Sources Chrétinnes.* Series. Paris: Les Éditions du cerf, 1968.

SC   "Sacrosanctum Concilium." Sacrosanctum Concilium Oecumenicum Vaticanum II. *AAS* 56 (1964): 97-138.

SL   *Studia Liturgica.*

S.Car   *Sacramentum Caritatis,* post-synodal apostolic exhortation of Pope Benedict XVI on the Eucharist as the Source and Summit of the Church's Life and Mission, February 22, 2007.

Tanner   Tanner, N. P. ed. *Decrees of the Ecumenical Councils.* With Latin and English Texts. 2 Volumes. London: Shed & Ward Ltd, 1990.

INTRODUCTION

The new Roman Missal that we attempt to explain in this book is the third typical edition of the Roman Missal (*Missale Romanum – editio typica tertia*) promulgated by Pope John Paul II in the Jubilee Year 2000 and published in 2002. The English translation of this Missal is coming very soon. For a long time the English speaking believers have used and heard the words of the Missal which is the translation of the two previous editions of the post-Vatican II Missal in 1970 and 1975 respectively. Therefore, when the translation of the new Missal is introduced in the parishes, Catholics will hear some new words or expressions in the Holy Mass celebrated according to the Roman Rite. In this context, it becomes necessary to understand whether the new Missal is in conformity with the Tradition of the Church as a form of authentic progress.

This book highlights how the new Missal follows the two principles for liturgical reform set forth by Vatican II: "sound Tradition" and "legitimate progress."[1] The new Missal includes several additions and modifications in rubrics as well as texts. In order to understand and appreciate the new Missal, first of all we have set it in the historical and theological context of the Tradition of the Church. This historical and theological perspective will assist believers to see how the Church, the bride of Christ has tried to give perfect expressions in her prayer during every century according to the contemporary needs guided by the indwelling of the Holy Spirit. With this background it would be easier to observe the modifications and additions in the various prayers of the new Roman Missal and discuss their significance and usefulness in pastoral circumstances.

---

[1] SC #23. See also A. Bugnini, *The Reform of the Liturgy 1948-1975*, trans. Mathew J. O'Connell (Collegeville, MN.: The Liturgical Press, 1983), 42-43. "Sound Tradition" means rooted in the Tradition of the Church and "legitimate progress" means bringing the text relevant for the contemporary context.

Before we begin to understand the changes in the new Missal and its vernacular translation, two popular misunderstandings about the Missal should be clarified. First of all, occasionally we hear people expressing concern that the new Missal is going to replace the Mass celebrated in English at present and mandate that in future Mass should be celebrated only in Latin. This is not true. The new edition of the Roman Missal was published in Latin already in 2002 and it has been translated into several languages in the world. The new edition of the Missal that we consider at present is going to be in English and not in Latin; it is a translation of the Latin Missal just as the previous ones, which are currently in use. The Roman Missal is always written in Latin first then translated into vernacular. The second misunderstanding is that some express worries that the introduction of changes in the prayers will cause confusion; hence postpone the introduction of the new edition of the Roman Missal. This fear is unfounded if one understands the history and content of the Missal. In the history of the Church there have been several revisions of the liturgical books and this new edition also fits into that pattern. The new Missal has been enriched in content, deeply rooted in Scripture and theology. The Missal has gone through a maze of discussions nationally and internationally with representatives from all English speaking countries, with experts in various fields, and bishops. One will find it instrumental to pray and articulate faith with better expressions rooted in Scripture and Christian Tradition. However, our human experience teaches us that introduction of any thing new including a new car or appliance would cause some initial discomfort which will be eventually overcome when one wholeheartedly begins to use it. Similarly, the new translation may sound different initially, which can be easily overcome with appropriate catechesis on the Missal and active participation in the celebration of the Holy Mass.

This book has six chapters. The first chapter examines the historical context of the Roman Missal. Historical knowledge helps us to appreciate how the same expressions are preserved in the prayer of the Church for so many centuries and how through the use of those words we too share the wealth of the spiritual experiences of our ancestors in faith from the early days of Christianity. The second chapter explains the evolution of MR 2002 and highlights some salient features of the General Instruction of the Roman Missal which is the first part of the Missal. The third chapter offers information on various parts of the Mass and their theological and liturgical significance. The fourth chapter explains the noticeable changes in the translation and their implication. The fifth chapter examines some examples of significant textual and rubrical modification and their relevance in the liturgy. The final chapter presents a schema for liturgical catechesis, which this book hopes will assist the pastors, deacons, various ministers who assist in liturgy, religious educators, and lay faithful at the introduction of the Missal in their respective parishes so that the new Missal becomes instrumental in bringing liturgical renewal.

CHAPTER I

HISTORICAL AND THEOLOGICAL CONTEXTS OF THE ROMAN MISSAL

The earliest apostolic testimonies acknowledge the Eucharist as the essential mark of Christian identity: "They devoted themselves to the apostles' teaching and fellowship, to the breaking of bread and the prayers" (Acts 2: 42). Thus the command of the Lord at the Last Supper to "Do this in remembrance of me" (Lk 22:19) was faithfully continued by the Christian communities (Acts 2:46, 20:7-11) where they recognized the presence of the Risen Lord (Lk 24:31). The early Christians did not use any Sacramentary or Missal for the celebration of Eucharist. For example, the *Didache*, an early Christian record from the second century admonishes: "Allow the prophets to give thanks (*eucharistein*) as much as they wish."[2] Similarly the writings of St. Justin and *The Apostolic Tradition* generally attributed to Hippolytus also acknowledge a spontaneous thanksgiving at the liturgy where improvisation was the rule,[3] but always conforming to the tradition received through the apostles. During the fourth and fifth centuries, several historical and theological factors contributed towards regulation in the use of texts during liturgy giving rise to liturgical books in the subsequent periods. Among various reasons, the growing number of heresies and poor quality of prayers composed by priests and bishops were the most compelling rationale for the codification of the liturgical texts. Such codification offered advantage over oral transmission of texts used for worship. The orthodoxy was defined through well formulated liturgical texts.

---

[2] *Didache* 10,7. quoted in H. Bettenson, ed., *The Early Christian Fathers* (Oxford: Oxford University Press, 1978), 51.

[3] L. Bouyer, "L'improvisation liturgique dans l'Eglise ancienne," LMD 111 (1972): 7-19. See also C. Hanson, "The Liberty of the Bishop to Improvise Prayer in the Eucharist," Vigiliae Christianne 15 (1969): 173-176; S. J. Lionel, *Let Us Celebrate* (Bangalore, India: Asian Trading Corporation, 2006), 13.

Christian leaders felt the need to check the content of the orations used during liturgy.[4] For example, St. Augustine, bishop of Hippo complained against the quality of clergy's improvisation and protested certain bishops who used the prayers composed by incompetent authors and heretics. Some African synods during the same period forbade the use of liturgical formularies which were not approved by the synods. From the fourth and fifth centuries the intervention of local synods became evident leading to slow emergence of uniform texts in prayer. Nevertheless, this uniformity remained within the regions. This trend towards uniformity produced two results: 1) preserving orthodoxy in the teaching of the Church and 2) maintaining good quality of prayers used in the liturgy.[5]

1. The Texts Known as *Libelii*

Libelii are small books more like pamphlets with only a few pages containing some liturgical texts. These are collection of formularies for one or several masses or various occasions. Although *Libelii* are not liturgical books as such they serve as an intermediary link in the transition from the period of improvisation to the formulation of the liturgical book, properly so called. Nonetheless, the first liturgical books are nothing but a collection of several *libelii*, which were formerly independent from one another. *Libelii* were organized with homogeneous content which served as antecedents for later development of sacramentaries and missals. Several studies on *libelii* shed light on the different forms of Christian worship in the early centuries.[6]

---

[4] M. Vos, "A la recherche de normes pour les textes liturgiques de la messe (V^e – VIIe siècle)," *Revue d'Historie ecclesiastique* 69 (1974): 5-37.

[5] A. Bouley, "From Freedom to Formula: The Evolution of the Eucharistic Prayer from Oral Improvisation to Written Texts," *Studies in Christian Antiquity* 21 (Washington, D.C., 1981).

[6] E. Palazzo, "Le role des *libelii* dans la pratique liturgique du haut Moyen Age: Histoire et typologie," *Revue Mabillon* 62/1 (1990): 9-36.

2. Development of Sacramentary

In the West, the liturgical books containing the presidential prayers[7] of the liturgy are known as Sacramentaries, while in the East a similar collection of prayers are known as Euchologies. Thus in the Western Rites, the term Sacramentary is associated with the collection of prayers for the Mass.[8] Since the scope of this book is the Roman Missal, examination of sacramentaries are necessary to understand these antecedents of the Missal. Although there are several sacramentaries, each of which could be subject of detailed study, this book will give brief background of the major sacramentary traditions only. This section offers background on some sacramentaries from where the Roman Missal of 2002 has borrowed prayers that were modified according to contemporary context.

2.1. Leonine Sacramentary

Leonine Sacramentary is one of the oldest sacramentaries which is generally believed to be from the fifth century. Though the original Leonine Sacramentary remained in manuscript form, it was printed for the first time only in 1735 by the effort of G. Blanchini. He attributed this sacramentary to Pope Leo (440-461) and gave the title "Old Sacramentary of the Roman Church Composed by Pope St. Leo I." However later studies revealed that this sacramentary was not entirely composed by Pope Leo I personally

---

[7] Presidential Prayers refer to the prayers said by priests during liturgy.

[8] C. Vogel, *Medieval Liturgy: An Introduction to the Sources,* trans. W. G. Storey and N. K. Rasmussen (Washington DC.: The Pastoral Press, 1981), 64-106. See also *Encyclopedia of Early Christianity,* 810; D. M. Hope, *The leonine Sacramentary: A Reassessment of its Nature and Purpose* (Oxford: Oxford University Press, 1971), 16, 23; C. L. Feltoe, *Sacramentarium Leonianum: Edited with Introduction, Notes and Three Photographs* (Cambridge: University Press, 1896), viii; H. A. Wilson, *The Gregorian Sacramentary Under Charles the Great,* xviff; H. A. Wilson, *The Gelasian Sacramentary: Edited with Introduction, Critical Notes and Appendix* (Oxford: Clarendon Press, 1894), xviii.

but it may contain some prayers composed by him. In the light of similar studies, J. Assemani rectified the previous erroneous title in 1749 and called his edition "Sacramentary of Verona," because it is a manuscript written in Verona in the first quarter of the seventh century after the ancient Roman model (c. 5th century) which is lost. It is preserved in Verona to this day.[9] In the fifth century each stational church in Rome had its own booklet for Mass (*libellus missarum*), presenting orations for solemnities and saints associated with that church. The Leonine Sacramentary, preserved in Verona manuscript from early 7th century, is actually the 6th century collection of these individual booklets (*libelli*).[10] L. C. Mohlberg has showed that large portion of the beginning of the sacramentary is missing and all the visible traces of the collection of *libelii* and the origin of the book have disappeared.[11]

Leonine Sacramentary contains 1331 prayers mainly orations and prefaces for various Masses. These prayers are not organized for the direct use in the liturgical celebrations because the prayers are arranged according to civil calendar and not liturgical year. The plan in the critical editions published indicates that each month included several formularies for the same feast. Hence scholars like Palazzo argue that it was a careless compilation of *libelii*. This observation explains why Leonine Sacramentary did not have any direct descendent and was quickly replaced by more thoroughly organized works such as Gelasian and Gregorian Sacramentaries.

---

[9] E. Palazzo, *A History of Liturgical Books from the Beginning to the Thirteenth Century*, trans. M. Beaumont (Collegeville, MN.: The Liturgical Press, 1998), 39.

[10] *Encyclopedia of Early Christianity*, 810; D. M. Hope, *The leonine Sacramentary: A Reassessment of its Nature and Purpose* (Oxford: Oxford University Press, 1971), 16, 23; C. L. Feltoe, *Sacramentarium Leonianum: Edited with Introduction, Notes and Three Photographs* (Cambridge: University Press, 1896), viii.

[11] L. C. Mohlberg, ed., *Sacramentarium Veronense* (Rome, 1955). See also J. Pinell I Pons, "Teologia e liturgia negli scritti S. Leone Magno," EO 8 (1991): 137-181.

Nevertheless, Leonine Sacramentary is important from historical and liturgical perspectives, because it sheds light on worship in the city of Rome in the early days and it is the only material witness for the transition from improvisation to codification through liturgical books. Liturgical research has identified that a great part of its contents are found in the later sacramentaries in a different form of organization and arrangement. As Vogel[12] and Palazzo[13] observe, until recently liturgical historians believed that the various types of sacramentaries succeeded one another in time, whereas in fact they exchanged material, influenced one another, and appeared roughly at the same time within different settings of celebration such as papal or presbyterial.

2.2. The Gelasian Sacramentaries

The Gelasian Sacramentary serves as the earliest agent for development of prayers in the other sacramentaries of the Roman rite, including the present Roman Missal. Proper understanding of this sacramentary presupposes clarification of two popular misunderstanding about Gelasian Sacramentaries. First of all this sacramentary was originally attributed to Pope Gelasius (492-496), however later studies revealed that Gelasius was not the author. Nevertheless the prayers composed by Gelasius are preserved in this sacramentary. Gelasius was also author of certain prayers found in Leonine Sacramentary. Secondly, for a long time liturgical historians failed to identify two types of Gelasian sacramentaries: the Old Gelasian Sacramentary and the Eighth-Century Gelasian which is also known as Frankish-Gelasian. The entries in library catalogues indicate that during the middle ages they were not aware of these two types. Hence it is important to explain these types of Gelasian Sacramentaries which had influence on the Post-Tridentine Missal[14] as well as Post-Vatican II editions of the Roman Missal.[15]

---

[12] C. Vogel, *Medieval Liturgy*, 62-63.

[13] E. Palazzo, *A History of Liturgical Books*, 42.

[14] MR 1570.

[15] MR 1970, MR 1975, MR 2002.

2.2.1. The Old Gelasian

The Gelasian Sacramentary appears to be the first true liturgical book in a real sense of the term with good organization of prayers together with evangeliaries (scripture readings). It appears to be Roman through and through. Its title sentence, "Here begins the sacramentary of the Roman Church ordered according to the yearly cycle" and its Sanctoral with the list of Roman saints confirm its Roman origin. The Old Gelasian Sacramentary was published for the first time in 1680 by Cardinal Tomasi. Ever since, it received great attention in numerous liturgical studies. The Old Gelasian Sacramentary has 1704 prayers divided into three distinct sections (or books): 1) celebrations of the Temporal from Nativity to Pentecost, 2) Sanctoral and one common of Saints as well as Advent Masses, 3) Masses for Ordinary Sundays, Canon of the Mass, and a series of Votive Masses. The standard formulary of this sacramentary is made up of two collects, one secret, a proper preface, a post-communion prayer and one prayer over the people (*oratio super populum*).

Liturgical historians testify that the Old Gelasian Sacramentary appears to be the earliest agent of the Romanization of the Frankish liturgy before the reform of Pepin the Short (751-768). This Old Gelasian, which was used in the presbyterial churches of Rome during seventh and eight centuries, gradually made its way into Gaul through the pilgrims who visited Rome. When this sacramentary reached beyond the Alps it was gallicanized by insertion of five sections which are of Frankish in origin. These are attested by the documents on liturgy in Gaul before the introduction of the Roman book. The five Frankish sections added to the Gelasian concern rituals for various occasions: ordinations, consecration virgins, dedication of a church, blessing of the lustral water and funeral.

2.2.2. The Eighth-Century Gelasian or Frankish Gelasian

The English liturgist E. Bishop uses the expression "Roman Sacramentary of King Pepin" to designate the Eighth-Century

Gelasians. There are dozens of manuscript evidences to prove its Frankish origin. As identified by scholars like Palazzo,[16] its archetypes can be recovered through the Gellone Sacramentary written about 790-800 perhaps in Meaux.[17] The later Eighth-Century Gelasians are the result of systematic revision of the Gellone Sacramentary.[18] The Eighth-Century Gelasians manifest monastic influence since several rites used exclusively for monasteries are found in them. The Sanctoral of Old Gelasian was adapted to include many Gallican saints. Hence it is probable that King Pepin used the monks to help in the compilation of this sacramentary as a part of his ambitious project of liturgical unification in his kingdom. During the compilation of the Eighth-Century Gelasians, the monks used two sources: the Old Gelasian and the type 2 Gregorian (*Paduense*) which was a papal sacramentary modified for presbyterial use. Frankish-Gelasian is the first major attempt of liturgical unification undertaken by royal authority. The number of copies circulated in his kingdom proves its success. However the success was short-lived as it was supplanted by the Gregorian Sacramentary which Charlemagne obtained directly from Rome with the same intention of his father. The Eighth-Century Gelasian had considerable influence during the first decades of the ninth century to remedy deficiencies of the Gregorian Sacramentary.[19]

2.3. The Gregorian Sacramentaries

The Gelasian and Gregorian Sacramentaries constitute the two major sacramentary traditions that co-existed in Rome during 7th and 8th centuries. They were basis for later developments of other

---

[16] E. Palazzo, *A History of Liturgical Books*, 46.

[17] A. Dumas and J. Deshusses, eds., *Liber sacramentorum Gellonesis*, CCSL 159-159A (1981).

[18] Chavasses, "Le sacramentaire gélasien du VIIIe siècle: Ses deux principales formes," EL 73 (1959): 249-298.

[19] H. Barbe and J. Deshusses, "A la recherche du missel d'Alcuin," EL 82 (1968): 3-44.

liturgical texts. The Gregorian was not compiled by Pope St. Gregory. It was completed after him perhaps during the pontificate of Pope Honorius I (625-638), but it has orations, which may have been written by Gregory together with material from the 6th century sources common to Gelasian. The Gregorian Sacramentary is a book intended for the exclusive use of the pope perfectly organized according to the liturgical year: 83 formularies for the Temporal and 79 for the Sanctoral. During the second half of the seventh century Gregorian developed into three distinct directions, each one leading to different types of Gregorian Sacramentary: 1) the first type branched into two, one retained the papal character and developed into *Hadrianum* (one sent by the Pope to Charlemagne in 785), the other, together with the Gelasian, served as source for the 8th century Frankish-Gelasian sacramentary which in turn was used by Benedict of Aniane in his ninth-century supplement of Hadrianum;[20] 2) the second type was Padunese and 3) the third type was Pre-Hadrianic Gregorian.

2.3.1. The Gregorian of the Hadrianum

This title refers to the text sent by Pope Hadrian to Charlemagne between 784 and 791. Its contents are close to the book composed in the first half of the seventh century under Honorius I. The fusion of the Temporal and Sanctoral into one liturgical year distinguishes it from Gelasian. In Hadrianum the formularies present the following structure: one collect, one *super oblata* and one *ad complendum*, with very rare proper prefaces. While Gelasian had several proper prayers Gregorian limited the number of prayers. This is a fundamental difference that is continued later in the post-Tridentine and Post-Vatican II liturgical reforms. In the subsequent years historians have identified that the Gregorian Sacramentary

---

[20] *Encyclopedia of Early Christianity*, 810; H. A. Wilson, *The Gregorian Sacramentary Under Charles the Great*, xviff; H. A. Wilson, *The Gelasian Sacramentary: Edited with Introduction, Critical Notes and Appendix* (Oxford: Clarendon Press, 1894), xviii.

was steadily augmented by the additions to the liturgical year made by the popes Sergius I (687-701) and Gregory II (715-731).

After the liturgical unification of the Empire implemented by Charlemagne, Hadrianum was disseminated throughout the Empire. However very soon Hadrianum proved ill-adapted for the daily liturgy in the parishes, hence unsuited for the emperor's unification policy. Besides the unsuitability of Hadrianum in the parishes as brought out by the liturgists, the Emperor himself noticed some deficiencies in the book both in Latin language as well as its content. Soon under the patronage of the Emperor the liturgists decided to correct the text, then to augment it with a supplement so that it could serve for the daily liturgy in parishes. Thus resulted what is called Supplement to Hadrianum, which is also known as *Supplementum*. In the past this Supplement was attributed to Alcuin, a masterful Carolingian liturgist to whom we owe the composition of many votive Masses and even a sacramentary.[21] However, modern liturgical historians agree that it was Benedict of Aniane (750-821) who was mastermind of the Supplement to Hadrianum.[22]

The Supplement contains two parts: 1) many formularies arranged according to the liturgical year, that were missing in Hadrianum (Sundays after Christmas, after Epiphany, after Easter, after Ascension, after Pentecost, Common of Saints, certain votive Masses, various blessings, consecrations and ordinations for the use of monastics, the *ordo* of baptism, the whole of Ordinary Sundays and so on); 2) two-hundred and twenty-one proper prefaces, a series of blessings given by the bishop and ritual for the ordinations to minor orders. In this enormous revision of the Gregorian Sacramentary primarily three sources were used: 1) the Old Gelasian, 2) the Type 2 Gregorian, which was used for presbyterial liturgy,

---

[21] J. Deshusses and H. Barre, "A la recherche du missel d'Alcuin," EL 82 (1968): 3-44.

[22] J. Deshusses, "Le supplement au sacramentaire Gregorian: Alcuin ou saint Benoit d'Aniane?" *Archiv fur Liturgiewissenschaft* 9 (1965): 48-71.

and 3) Frankish-Gelasian. Besides these primary sources, several other sources of Roman and Frankish origin contributed to enrich the content of the Supplement. The descendents of Hadrianum are numerous since this book was the point of departure for the evolution from sacramentary to present day Roman Missal.[23] By the end of the ninth century, Supplement to Hadrianum was used throughout the West for the large part. The number of its manuscripts testifies to the success of this Supplement to Hadrianum.

2.3.2. Paduense

The Sacramentary known as Paduense is a single manuscript copied in the middle of the ninth century, perhaps in Padua in northern Italy. The contents of Paduense suggest that it is a revision of the Gregorian executed between 659 and 681 in order to adapt the papal sacramentary to presbyterial use which is classified by liturgical historians as Type 2 Gregorian. Although the liturgical historians and experts in manuscripts have not identified any direct descent of this sacramentary, one can surmise that the compilers of the Eighth-Century Gelasian and later on, the Supplement to Hadrianum used Paduense as one of their sources in the composition.[24]

2.3.3. The Pre-Hadrianic Gregorian

Scholars such as Deshusses have proved that even before the Gregorian was sent by Hadrian at the request of Charlemagne, the Gregorian Sacramentary reached Gaul at the end of the eighth century.[25] This copy of the Gregorian was composed about 685 on the foundation of primitive Gregorian. The contents of Pre-Hadrianic Gregorian circulated in Gaul reveal the state of Hadrianum before

---

[23] A. Dumas, "Les sources du nouveau missel romain," *Notitae* (1971): 37ff. See also P. Bruylants, *Les oraisons du missel romain,* 2 vols. (Luvain, 1952).

[24] E. Palazzo, *A History of Liturgical Books,* 54.

[25] J. Deshusses, "Le sacramentaire gregorien pre-hadrianique," *Revue benedictine* 80 (1970): 213-237.

the additions made by Sergius I. It was probably written for Arno, bishop of Salzburg in 825. He was a close friend of Alcuin. Although this Pre-Hadrianic Gregorian does not have any direct descendants, its contents were used to compose a sacramentary to be used in his abbey of St. Martin. It is also known as Alcuin's Missal. Scholars were able to reconstruct his Missal from two sacramentaries dating back to ninth century: Sacramentary of Tours and Sacramentary of Trent.[26]

2.4. Composite Sacramentaries

Examination of the evolution of sacramentaries revealed how one text influenced the other across the geographical boundaries and various sources of their origin. The grand composition and success of supplemented Hadrianum was not the final stage in the evolution of sacramentaries. During the second half of the ninth century the fusion of Hadrianum with its supplement warranted some rearrangement which resulted in a few additions and textual remodeling. The result of this remodeling was called "composite sacramentaries" by the liturgical historians, because these composite sacramentaries included prayers from various sacramentaries of Gelasian and Gregorian traditions. For example, the Sacramentary of Fulda was composed as composite sacramentary in 975. It was copied and decorated in Fulda for export to other regions. It stands as a true liturgical "monument" to the glory of the Carolingian past and its sacramentaries. This sacramentary is also characterized with extravagant number of orations, much too large for daily liturgical use in parishes. It also proves the desire of that period not to lose any of those prayers which have come through a long tradition.[27]

---

[26] J. Deshusses, "Le sacramentaire gregorien de Trente," *Revue benedictine* 78 (1968): 261-282.

[27] E. Palazzo, *A History of Liturgical Books*, 56.

3. From Sacramentary to Missal

The liturgical historians observe that during the tenth and eleventh centuries there was progressive disappearance of sacramentaries and steady appearance of the Missal.[28]

3.1. Fusion into One Volume

Sacramentary, Lectionary, and Antiphonal came to be united in one volume known as Missal, which became convenient for the use in daily liturgy. In the middle ages it was expressed by the term "complete missal" (*missale completum* or *missale plenarium*). This fusion of different books into one missal came through different stages and coexisted side by side for centuries.

3.1.1. Stages of Fusion

Historians categorize four stages of this fusion that provide a systematic understanding of the emergence of the Missal: 1) From the ninth century, marginal notes were added to sacramentaries indicating beginning (*incipit*) of the chants taken from Antiphonal, 2) Collection of prayers for certain feasts, votive Masses or other special occasions were put together with readings and chants. They were called *Libelli missarum*, which was the antecedent of "complete missal," 3) Juxtapositioning different books such as sacramentary, lectionary, antiphons and various other combinations as one volume binding, and 4) Integrated Mass book with orations, readings, and chants all inserted in their proper place according to the order of the Mass. This fourth stage development of the Missal as complete book became more numerous than sacramentaries toward the end of ninth century. The popularity of Missal grew so much that by the fourteenth century sacramentaries became merely an archaic remnant.[29] Ever since, the Mass book is known as the

---

[28] Ibid, 55.

[29] C. Folsom, "Liturgical Books of the Roman Rite," in *Handbook for Liturgical Studies* vol 1 "Introduction to the Liturgy" ed. A. J. Chupungco (Collegeville, MN.: The Liturgical Press, 1997), 262-264.

Roman Missal (*Missale Romanum*), including our present time. That is why new translations of the Missal call it Roman Missal and not Sacramentary. As explained in this chapter the present Mass book is not sacramentary with fragments of prayers but complete collection of all the prayers and well organized, hence the title Roman Missal is more fitting than Sacramentary.

3.1.2. Reasons for Fusion

Liturgical historians identify four reasons for the fusion of all the prayers as one Missal: 1) development of private Mass, 2) obligation on the part of priests to recite all the parts of the Mass, 3) pastoral usefulness especially in the parishes far away from diocesan or monastic centers, and 4) influence of priestly piety and concern to omit nothing.[30]

3.2. Stages in the Development of Missal

Generally historians sketch four stages of development in the history of the Roman Missal: 1) the Gregorian-Gelasian synthesis from ninth to twelfth centuries, 2) various traditions of the thirteenth century, 3) the post-Tridentine Missal, and 4) the post-Vatican II Missal.

3.2.1. Gregorian-Gelasian Synthesis

The fusion of sacramentary and antiphons had its origin in the Franco-Roman synthesis described earlier through the agent of Frankish-Gelasian or the Eighth-Century Gelasian Sacramentary. With the advent of the Supplement to Gregorian there was a new synthesis of the Gregorian/Supplement and Frankish-Gelasian. One must remember that the authentic Roman tradition in the form of Gelasian and Gregorian in essence was preserved in the multiple combinations of sources. These combined sources serve as bridge between the Hadrianum and the Roman Missal used by the Roman Curia in 1474. The same sources had influence on the Roman Missal

---

[30] P. Borella, "Verso il messale plenario," EL 67 (1953): 338-340.

of 1570 by Pope Pius V and all the editions of the Roman Missals after Vatican II.

3.2.2. Various Traditions of the Thirteenth Century

During the thirteenth century the city of Rome knew four liturgical customs: 1) the papal court, 2) St. Peter's in the Vatican , 3) the reform of Cardinal Orsini (later Pope Nicholas III), 4) the Lateran Basilica.

(1) The papal court resided at the Lateran Palace, usually celebrating the liturgy in the pope's private chapel. The tradition of the papal court underwent four distinct phases during the thirteenth century: a) Innocent III reorganized the Divine Office but Mass was untouched, b) Honorius III revised the Office again. Though he did not revise Mass, he issued the Missal. This Missal of Honorius was adapted by Franciscans in 1230 and was known as *Regula Missale*. C) The Missal of Honorius was once again revised in 1240, d) Regula books were also revised in 1243-1244.

(2) The books from St. Peter's Basilica in Rome represent the Old-Roman rite used for centuries which are different from the books of the papal court. Other churches in the city also followed the Old-Roman rite.

(3) In the mid 1250s the liturgy of the papal court was making serious inroads into the tradition of the city. John Cardinal Orsini, later Pope Nicholas III resisted such change, and in an effort to save the urban rite he devised a compromise: a new urban liturgy which combined the urban and papal rites, that is, the tradition of St. Peter's Basilica and Lateran Basilica were combined. Since Nicholas III died in 1280, and the confusion caused due to transfer of papacy to Avignon, this local reform did not bring any result.

(4) The Lateran Basilica had its own liturgical tradition distinct from papal court.

These four liturgical traditions, all of them authentically Roman, influenced each other during the thirteenth century. During such mutual influence, ultimately the papal tradition dominated and other urban traditions eventually disappeared. In this context the papal Missal adapted by Franciscans was revised and approved by Clement V (1305-1314) and adapted for the papal chapel. This Missal was the basis for the first printed Missal of 1474 used by the Roman Curia.[31] In most part it was adapted by Pius V after the Council of Trent.

3.2.3. Post-Tridentine Missal

Since the Missal had already undergone so many revisions was there need for yet another new Missal after the Council of Trent? Liturgical reform was necessary after the Council of Trent because there was a still enormous variety of texts from one diocese to another and in many instances within a diocese itself, which caused confusion and led to many abuses. The Council of Trent, in Session twenty-five (1552) discussed the liturgical reform. A commission was formed under the guidance of Archbishop Leonardo Marini. Since the members of the commission could not agree upon the criteria to adopt for the liturgical reform and since it was necessary to bring the council to a close, the project to reform was turned over to Pope Pius IV (1559-1565). After the death of Pius IV, this project was passed on to his successor Pope Pius V who added new members to the commission and finally the revised Missal was promulgated in 1570. The research by Frutaz has shown that Guglielmo Cardinal Sirleto was instrumental in the liturgical reform following the directives of the Council.[32]

---

[31] C. Folsom, "Liturgical Books of the Roman Rite," 266.

[32] Ibid.

The missal of Pius V was little more than a re-edition[33] of what was already in use by the Roman curia in 1474.[34] Scholars such as Pietro Sorci,[35] Adrien Nocent,[36] and Marcel Metzger conclude that the *Missale Romanum* of 1570 came to be known as "missal of Pius V" only because he promulgated it. They point out that in reality this missal existed a century earlier.[37] In the words of Ratzinger:

> The Missal, which appeared in 1570 by order of Pius V, differed only in tiny details from the first printed edition of the Roman Missal of about a hundred years earlier. Basically, the reform of Pius V was only concerned with eliminating certain late

---

[33] *Missalis Romani; Editio Princeps Mediolani Anno 1474 prelis mandata,* Introduction by A. Ward and C. Johnson (Roma: C.L.V. Edizioni Liturgiche, 1996), XIV-XVIII.

[34] The liturgical reform of Pius V is not an isolated event in 1570 born out of pope's own initiative, but it has to be understood in the historical and theological context of almost a century earlier. Before Gutenberg's invention of printing press, missals were hand-copied by monk, cleric or professional copyist for a particular cathedral, parish, or chapel. They had sufficient knowledge in the field and were controlled only by customary laws. There were very few ecclesiastical laws that governed such copying of liturgical texts. Canon Robert Amiet's research on twenty-two pre-Tridentine missals revealed ninety-three variants in the mass. Cf. J. M. Pommares, "The Origins of the Roman Missal in the Liturgical works of Pope Pius V" *Theological and Historical Aspects of the Roman Missal: Proceedings of the Fifth International Colloquium* (Kingston and Surbiton, UK: CIEL, 2000), 165-179.

[35] P. Sorci, "Il Messale Romano come strumento della tradizione celebrative," in C. Giraudo, ed., *Il Messale Romano: Tradizione, traduzione, adattamento,* Associazione Professori di Liturgia XXX settimana di studio, Gazzada 2002 (Roma: Edizioni Liturgiche, 2003), 45-47.

[36] A. Nocent, *La célébration eucharistique avant et après saint Pie V* (Paris: Beauchesne, 1977), 44-45.

[37] M. Metzger, *History of the Liturgy: The major stages,* trans. Madeleine Beaumont (Collegeville, MN.: The Liturgical Press, 1997), 128.

medieval accretions and the various mistakes and misprints, which had crept in.[38]

Redaction studies[39] reveal that Pius V borrowed prefaces from the Gregorian sacramentary.[40] The new prefaces added in MR 1570 (e.g.: Epiphany and Ascension) are slightly modified versions from the Gelasian sacramentary.[41] Through these prayers in the Missal, Pius V intended to defend the doctrines enshrined in the liturgy, especially those concerning the sacrificial nature of the Mass, the ministerial priesthood, and the real presence of Christ.[42] While Liturgical historians draw our attention to some of the lacunæ, amplifications and overlapping rituals in MR 1570,[43] nevertheless, when one observes the post-reformation context of the missal one must acknowledge that the prayers were helpful in preserving doctrinal unity in the Church. Cipriano Vagaggini shows this clearly

---

[38] J. Ratzinger, *The Feast of Faith: Approaches to a Theology of the Liturgy*, trans. G. Harrison (San Francisco: Ignatius Press, 1986), 85-86.

[39] P. Sorci, 48-56.

[40] H. Ashworth, "I nuovi prefazi," RL, 6 (1968): 758-781.

[41] P. Bruylants, LMD 87 (1966): 111. Prefaces for Epiphany, Ascension are new in MR 1570.

[42] Tanner, vol. 2, 733-734. See also GIRM #7 in LDS II, 9. See also A. G. Martimort, ed., "The Eucharist" *The Church at Prayer*, vol. 2, trans. M. J. O'Connell (Collegeville, MN.: The Liturgical Press, 1986), 176.

[43] R. Cabie, "The Celebration of the Eucharist in the West from the Council of Trent to Vatican Council II," in A. G. Martimort, ed., *The Church at Prayer*, vol. 2, 175, 133-142. See also K. J. Coyle, "From Homily to Sermon to Homily: The content of Christian liturgical preaching in historical perspective," *Liturgical ministry*, 15 (Winter 2006): 6; John Harper, *The Forms and Orders of Western Liturgy from tenth to eighteenth century* (New York: Oxford University Press, 1991), 156, 164.

The use of vernacular language was not allowed by the Council of Trent as it was thought by the council Fathers not the opportune time due to rebellion of reformers against the use of Latin in the liturgy. Cf. N. Tanner, 732.

when highlighting the importance given to the text of the Roman Canon in defending the doctrine against the attacks from Protestants.[44] After Pius V, the Missal received minor modifications such as rubrical adjustments, additions of formularies for the newly canonized saints and additions of four new prefaces under Clement VIII (1604), Urban VIII (1634), and Benedict XV (1920).

3.2.4. Post-Vatican II Missal

Annibale Bugnini[45] rightly observed in his book that the Second Vatican Council's reform is differentiated from all other reforms in the history of the liturgy by its pastoral emphasis.[46] The important purpose of the liturgical reform was to rejuvenate and update the expression of the Church's liturgy in its entirety, in words, actions and gestures. In the words of Pope Pius XII, the liturgical reform was a "movement of the Holy Spirit in the Church."[47]

3.2.4.1. Result of the Liturgical Movement

The effort originated with Abbot Prosper Guéranger (d. 1875)[48] which later came to be known as Liturgical Movement was an effort

---

[44] C. Vagaggini, "Le Canon Roman et la réforme liturgique," LMD 87 (1966): 134.

[45] He was secretary of the Consilium for the implementation of the *Sacrosanctum Concilium* (1964-1969) and secretary of the Congregation for Divine Worship (1969-1975).

[46] A. Bugnini, *The Reform of the Liturgy*, 5. See also. A. G. Martimort, *The Church at Prayer,* vol.2, 191.

Bugnini was also secretary of the commission for liturgical reform under Pius XII (1948), secretary for the preparation commission on liturgy (1960-1962), *peritus* of the Second Vatican Council and of its commission of the liturgy.

[47] A. Bugnini, *The Reform of the Liturgy*, xxvi.

[48] Though Guéranger took bold initiative towards liturgical movement the origin could be even traced back to Pius IX who wanted to revise the Thomistic approach to theology.

to reunite rites and content in the Roman liturgy, restoring the sanctifying power of liturgy and bringing the faithful back to full participation and understanding. Pius X in his *motu proprio "Tra le Sollecitudini"* (1903) viewed the active participation of the faithful in the liturgy as the primary and important source of true Christian spirit.[49] This *stimuli* given by Pius X was taken seriously by Dom Lambert Beauduin from the Abbey of Mont-Cesar who started the organized liturgical movement in 1909, followed by the Benedictines of Maria Laach in Germany sourcing on deep biblical, patristic and theological aspects of liturgy and with pastoral effectiveness as its goal.[50] Through *Mediator Dei,* the encyclical letter of Pius XII (1947) the liturgical movement received its official seal. The idea of reform acquired definite shape when the task was assigned to the Sacred Congregation for Rites. In 1948, a commission for liturgical reform was appointed with Cardinal Clemente Micara, prefect of the Sacred Congregation of Rites, as its president.

Another force that was operative in ensuring liturgical reform was the International Congress of Pastoral Liturgy. It gave the liturgy, a determining role in the Church's life and promoting the encounter of souls with God. During his address at this congress, Pius XII said, "The liturgical movement is ... a sign of the providential dispositions of God for the present time [and] of the movement of the Holy Spirit in the Church."[51]

---

[49] Pius X, motu proprio *Tra le Sollecitudini* (November 22, 1903), in A. Bugnini, ed., *Documenta Pontificia ad instaurationem liturgicam spectantia* (Rome, 1953) 12-13. English translation in J.J. Megivern (ed.), *Worship and Liturgy* (Wilmington, N.C., 1978) 17-18 (n. 28).

[50] The Sacerdotal Communities of St. Severin of Paris and St. Joseph of Nice, *The Liturgical Movement,* translated by Lancelot Sheppard (New York: Hawthorn Books, 1964), 34-35.

[51] *The Assisi Papers. Proceedings of the First International Congress of Pastoral Liturgy, Assisi-Rome, September 18-22, 1956* (Collegeville, MN.: 1957), 18-31.

3.2.4.2. Preparation for Liturgical Reform of Vatican II

Five months after the announcement of Vatican II on January 25, 1959, Pope John XXIII appointed Cardinal Cicognani as the president of the preparatory commission on the liturgy and Fr. Annibale Bugnini as the secretary. The initial presentation of the draft in the council entered a maze of theological discussions, suggesting amendments and corrections, which led to final approval and promulgation of the Constitution of the Sacred Liturgy on December 4, 1963 by Pope Paul VI after receiving 2147 voting in favor and four voting not in favor. The task of practical implementation of the liturgical constitution began immediately with the act of Pope Paul VI establishing *Consilium*. It was announced on January 25, 1964 in *motu proprio* "Sacram Liturgiam."[52]

3.2.4.3. The Task of the Consilium

The revision of the Roman Missal according to the letter and spirit of the *Sacrosanctum Concilium* was one of the most important tasks taken by the Consilium. After several sessions and discussions, the complete schema of the New Order of the Mass (*Novus Ordo Missæ*) was presented to the Consilium at its sixth general meeting, which was discussed at length with two experimental celebrations. It came to be known as "normative mass" because there would be several forms of celebration but this one should serve as standard or norm for others.[53] In 1966, Paul VI instructed the *Consilium* to send the liturgical schemas to the Synod of Bishops (1967) before which the *Consilium* was instructed to forward the texts to the bishops' conferences. The initial reaction to the experimental mass was rather negative. There were several sessions of experimental mass with various groups and even in the presence of the Pope.

---

[52] *AAS* 56 (1964) 140. Translated in *Documents on Liturgy. 1963-1979: Conciliar, Papal, and Curial Texts* (Collegeville, 1982) 20 nos. 276-289; see no. 278.

[53] A. Bugnini, *The Reform of the Liturgy*, 343.

After several lengthy discussions, amendments, and corrections, finally Paul VI promulgated *Missale Romanum* on April 28, 1969.

While commenting on some important features of the *Missale Romanum,* Bugnini made the following observation:

> …the Eucharistic prayers, anaphoras, and prefaces, all of which have been increased in number after the example of the Eastern liturgies, in order to give greater variety to the Church's prayer and to render the formulas more complete and richer in theological, scriptural, and liturgical content.[54]

When Pius V promulgated MR 1570, his intention was to provide the Christian people with an instrument of liturgical unity and an outstanding expression of the Church's authentic religious worship. In like manner, Paul VI, while acknowledging the legitimate variety and adaptations that characterize the new missal expects

> …that the faithful will receive the new missal as a help toward witnessing and strengthening their unity with one another; that through the new Missal one and the same prayer in a great diversity of languages will ascend, more fragrant than any incense, to our heavenly Father, through our High Priest, Jesus Christ, in the Holy Spirit.[55]

The Consilium for the Implementation of the Constitution of the Sacred Liturgy (CICSL) was divided into several working groups, each group bestowed with responsibility for reforming a particular area of the liturgy. For example, the group responsible for the reform of the Canon of the Mass was known as "Cœtus X." and the group responsible for preface[56] was known as "Cœtux XVIIIbis." Most

---

[54] A. Bugnini, *The Reform of the Liturgy*, 385. See also. Paul VI, Apostolic Constitution *Missale Romanum,* (3 April 1969) AAS 61 (1969) 217-222 in DOL 1358.

[55] A. Bugnini, *The Reform of the Liturgy*, 385.

[56] P. Bruylants, "Les Prefaces du missel romain," *La Maison-Dieu* 87 (1966), 111-133.

of these members had themselves been part of the liturgical movement, who had studied extensively the ancient liturgical sources especially the anaphora of both East and West.[57] Their liturgical spirituality was deeply rooted in the Mass celebrated by them according to Tridentine rite.[58] They looked into a wide variety of ancient sources within the Tradition of the Church while composing prayers for the new Missal after Vatican II.

3.2.4.4. Authentic Progress Rooted in Tradition

An examination of the sources of the new Missal reveals that the post-Tridentine and the post-Vatican II missals shared the same source as their starting point: "the tradition of the Fathers."[59] There were limitations and advantages in the respective reforms after Trent and Vatican II. If scholars after Trent had many obstacles, the context after Vatican II had the advantage of numerous discoveries, studies and critical editions of ancient sacramentaries published during the period between the two councils.

Pius V appointed a commission[60] to implement the directives of the Council of Trent with regard to reform of liturgy, but the commission had limited tools at its disposal.[61] Pius V in *Quo Primum*[62] acknowledged the restoration of the missal to be "...*ad pristinam ...sanctorum Patrum normam*" [according to the ancient... norm of the holy Fathers]. However, such "restoration"

---

[57] A. Detscher, "The Eucharistic Prayers of the Roman Catholic Church," in *New Eucharistic Prayers: An Ecumenical Study of their Development and Structure,* ed., Frank Senn (New York: Paulist Press, 1987), 19, 49.

[58] A. Ward, *Source Compendium*, 23, 30.

[59] GIRM #6 in LDS II, 8.

[60] It was presided by Cardinal Guglielmo Sirleto. Cf. T. Klauser, *A Short History of the Western Liturgy*, trans. J. Halliburton (London: Oxford University Press, 1969), 118.

[61] T. Klauser, *A Short History of the Western Liturgy*, 118.

[62] It promulgated the MR 1570 on 14 July 1570.

ad pristinam was far less than ideal since several ancient liturgical texts were yet to be discovered and critically analyzed.[63]

The following four examples help to understand the difficulty in reaching the ideal: 1) The codices of the Vatican library and the missal[64] had been printed for the first time only a century earlier in 1471,[65] 2) The printed versions of *Rituals* with some vernacular notes for catechetical purpose appeared only a few decades before the council,[66] 3) The ancient *Sacramentaries* and the *Ordines Romani* were not published until the 1700s,[67] and 4) Some of the ancient sacramentaries like the *Sacramentary of Padua, Hadrianum, Gelasian,* and *Gregorian* would not be critically analyzed until the 1900s.[68] The work of the Tridentine commission is to be applauded; it deserves merit for giving the Church a single, sure basis for its prayer purified of many transitory and imperfect elements. Nevertheless, the commission's vision of the "tradition"

---

[63] MR 1962, v. See also D. C. Smolarski, 6.

Although the manuscripts in the Vatican library provided material for the emendation of some expressions, they by no means made it possible to inquire into "ancient and approved authors" farther back than the liturgical commentaries of the middle ages. Cf. GIRM #7 and 9 in LDS II, 9-10.

[64] The missal refers to the missal that was used prior to 1570.

[65] *Missalis Romani: Editio Princeps Mediolani Anno 1474 prelis mandata,* Introduction by A. Ward and C. Johnson (Roma: C.L.V. Edizioni Liturgiche, 1996), XIV-XVIII.

[66] C. Vogel, *Medieval Liturgy,* 264.

[67] K. F. Pecklers, "History of the Roman Liturgy from the Sixteenth until the Twentieth Centuries," *Handbook for Liturgical Studies: Introduction to the Liturgy* vol. 1, ed. A. J. Chupungco (Collegeville, MN.: The Liturgical Press, 1997), 164. They were studied, and published with the initiative of scholars like Cardinal Giuseppe Tomasi. He died in 1713.

[68] C. Vogel, *Medieval Liturgy,* 118-119.

was necessarily limited[69] to "more recent tradition."[70] Most scholars agree that this understanding of tradition was in reaction to the Protestant Reformation.[71]

On the other hand, the publication of the critical editions of ancient sacramentaries during the interim period between the councils brought to light numerous prayers of no slight spiritual excellence that had previously been unknown. Similarly, the traditions dating back to the first centuries, even before the formation of the rites of East and West, became better known due to the discovery of several ancient liturgical manuscripts. The continuous progress in the study of the "holy Fathers" has also shed light upon the theology and mystery of Eucharist through their illustrations in their *mystagogia*. In such advantageous context, the *Consilium* after Vatican II was better able to go to the origins. It had access to the many forms of the Church's euchological riches.[72] It was able to benefit from the prolific research of the liturgical movement.[73] It enabled the reform to preserve not only the recent tradition but also to grasp the tradition of the very early days. This broad perspective "...allows us to see how the Holy Spirit endows the people of God with marvelous fidelity

---

[69] Ratzinger observes, "The Council limited itself deliberately to a rebuttal of Luther's negations in order to prepare the ground for theological discussion." Cf. J. Ratzinger, *Principles of Catholic Theology* (San Francisco: Ignatius Press, 1987), 263. For original title in German see *Theologische prinzipienlehre* (Munich: Erich Wewel Verlag, 1982).

[70] GIRM #7 and 9 in LDS II, 9-10.

[71] A. G. Martimort, ed., *The Church at Prayer*, vol. 2, 175-176.

[72] A. Bugnini observed, "The Eucharistic prayers, anaphoras, and prefaces, all of which have been increased in number after the example of the Eastern liturgies, in order to give greater variety to the Church's prayer and to render the formulas more complete and richer in theological, scriptural, and liturgical content." Cf. A. Bugnini, *The Reform of the Liturgy*, 385. See also Paul VI, Apostolic Constitution, *Missale Romanum,* (3 April 1969) AAS 61 (1969): 217-222 in DOL 1358.

[73] E. Palazzo, *A History of Liturgical Books*, 5, 10.

in preserving the unalterable deposit of faith, even amid a very great variety of prayers and rites."[74] Vatican II had the advantage of peace and tranquility to reflect on the pastoral needs of the faithful. The expression *resourcement*[75] does not imply archaeological reconstruction of the past.[76] This movement seeks to access sources in so far as this seems "useful or necessary"[77] so that the Church may celebrate the Paschal mystery in a worthy way. The positive contributions from the 1570 Missal have not been discarded, but preserved in many texts in the MR 2002,[78] which proves continuous fidelity in the liturgical tradition of the Church.

---

[74] GIRM #9 in LDS II, 10.

[75] This expression means return to the sources. It was a quest in the nineteenth century to study the sources in Scripture, patristic writings and liturgy.

[76] P. Bruylants explained to the members of *Cœtus* XVIIIbis that he was not advocating "archeologism" – that is, a preference for more ancient texts simply because they are ancient. Cf. *Schemata* n. 186, 2. It conforms with Pius XII's rejection of the same in *Mediator Dei* [AAS 39 (1947): 546-547]. Pius XII himself repeated this rejection of archeologism made by Pius VI in the 1794 Bull "Auctorem fidei." [*Schema* was working document prepared by experts in particular area. The initial work was scrutinized by sub commissions before presenting it to the liturgical commission. For more details on the organization of the various working groups of the *Concilium,* see A. Bugnini, *The Reform of the Liturgy,* 60-62, 67-68. See also P. M. Gy, *The Reception of Vatican II: Liturgical Reforms in the Life of the Church* (Milwaukee, WI.: Marquette University Press, 2003), 9; B. Botte, *Le Mouvement Liturgique: Témoniage et souvenirs* (Paris: Desclée, 1973), 156].

[77] SC #23, 50 in Flannery, 127, 135.

[78] SC #23, 50 in Flannery, 127, 135. See also A. G. Martimort, ed., *The Church at Prayer*, vol. 2, 193.

CHAPTER II

GENESIS OF THE THIRD TYPICAL EDITION OF THE ROMAN MISSAL AND ITS GENERAL INSTRUCTION

1. Promulgation of the *Editio Typica Tertia*

On 20th April 2000, Pope John Paul II promulgated the third typical edition of the Roman Missal,[79] which was published in 2002.[80] It is known as the third typical edition of the Roman Missal because there were already two editions of the Roman Missal after Vatican II, first in 1970 and second in 1975 respectively. MR 2002 is the result of the guidance of the Holy Spirit manifest in several years of intense study by the experts in liturgy, Roman Curia, and the Congregation for Divine Worship and Discipline of Sacraments. This MR 2002 is a linear development as a form of authentic progress from its previous editions after Vatican II. A brief survey of the evolution of the Roman Missal in the previous chapter has informed us that this sort of new edition after the liturgical reform is not something new in the history of the Church. For example, after the promulgation of the post-Tridentine Missal in 1570, the experts realized a need for some clarification in terminology and correction

---

[79] Henceforth the third typical edition of the Roman Missal 2002 will be referred as MR 2002 (*Missale Romanum* 2002).

[80] Missale Romanum *ex decreto Sacrosancti Oecumenici Concilii Vaticani II instauatum auctoritate Pauli PP.Vi promulgatum Ioannis Pauli PP. cura recognitum, Editio typica tertia* (Citta del Vaticano: Typis vaticanis, 2002). See also M. Lessi-Ariosto, *L' "editio typica tertia" del "Missale Romanum"*, in *Rivista Liturgica* 90 (2003): 501-512; *Notitiae* 38 (2002): 56-62.

of some expressions; hence a new edition was published in 1571.[81] History also informs us how this Missal of 1571 was renewed in subsequent years with new texts and addition of newly canonized saints after the Council of Trent. Similarly after years of strenuous work by the Consilium following the directives of Vatican II, the Missal was published in 1970. In order to incorporate some clarifications and corrections the second edition was published in 1975. For example, every preface in MR 1975 was given a summary subtitle which facilitates the priests to select them. The textual additions of MR 1975 include the following: several new Masses such as the Dedication of a Church, Dedication of an Altar, and in honor of Mary the Mother of the Church; and entrance and communion antiphons for Masses.[82] The English translation that is in use until now is the translation of the *Missale Romanum* 1975, *editio altera*; that is the second typical edition of the Roman Missal. Since there was already, a second edition in 1975 was it necessary for a third edition in 2002.

2. Necessity for New Edition of the Roman Missal

The revision of liturgical texts is not something new in the history of liturgy, because liturgy reflects the dynamic life of the Church and not static. At the same time, one should not misunderstand that a group of people can come together and create their own liturgy just because they want a new text since they are tired of the old one. In the history of the Church, three important

---

[81] P. Jounel, *Les rites de la messe en 1965: Les premières étapes de la réforme liturgique II – Textes, traduction, commentaire* (Paris: Centre de Pastorale liturgique, 1965), 13. Jounel cites L. Brou, *L'inclination de la tête au* Per eumdem Christum *du memento des morts, dans Miscellanea liturgica in bonorem, C. Mohlberg*, Rome 1948, pp. 1-31. See also P. Sorc, "Il messale romano come strumento della tradizione celebrative" in C. Giraudo, ed., *Il Messale Romano: Tradizione, traduzione, adattamento*, Associazione Professori di Liturgia XXX settimana di studio, Gazzada 2002 (Roma: Edizioni Liturgiche, 2003), 54.

[82] Notitae 11 (1975): 290-337.

theological and liturgical principles guide the revision of liturgical texts: 1) Due to the dynamic nature of liturgy itself any revision springs from within the Church as an organic development through an authentic ecclesial initiative guided by norms and directives. 2) The very structure of the liturgical year demands such revision, due to newly canonized saints. The liturgical year already has memorial for several saints, hence in order to accommodate the newly canonized saints, some of the feasts, memorials, or optional memorials are to be re-arranged. Hence, it calls for some revision through changes in the liturgical calendar, and composition of new prayers. 3) Revision also becomes necessary due to the need for enriching the liturgical prayers in the light of new studies and discoveries of ancient euchological treasures, new directives and laws by the Church, and genuine spiritual need of the culture of a particular time. If the principles mentioned above guide the liturgical revision in general, what are the specific needs that called for a new edition of the Roman Missal in 2002?

The third typical edition was necessary for various reasons as explained here below. First of all there was an urgent necessity to create this new edition of the Missal because there were so many changes in the Church during the period after the promulgation of the first edition after Vatican II in 1970 and 1975. Some of the prominent changes include the new Code of Canon law promulgated in 1983, documents, declarations by the Holy See, instructions and clarifications on liturgical matters issued by the congregation, new blessings approved, and Ordos for bishops, priest and deacons. In the light of all these new instructions, clarifications and directives, a new edition of the Roman Missal was necessary.

Secondly, learning from more than thirty years of liturgical renewal after Vatican II, it was the need of the hour. New prayers were added and rubrics were clarified to bring the emphasis of Vatican II. For example, the rubrical additions in the Lenten prefaces in MR 2002 better highlight the penitential and baptismal motifs insisted by Vatican II for the season of Lent. The whole idea behind the new edition is to make the new Missal easy to use in the light of interim changes after Vatican II and provide Roman Missal with more clarity.

Thirdly, in the context of numerous changes mentioned above there was a need for a pastorally friendly liturgical book that incorporates all these new directives and clarifications so that the pastors and people do not have the burden of checking the instructions when they use previous translations of the post-Vatican II missal. For example, the Eucharistic Prayers for the reconciliation and Masses with Children appeared provisionally in 1974 and were later approved for general use only after the 1975 Missal. The second edition of the Lectionary was revised and published in 1981 and the Ceremonial of Bishops was published in 1984. All these revisions have implication for the Roman Missal; hence new edition incorporating these changes was necessary.

Fourthly, the new edition is intended to contribute towards liturgical renewal and spiritual formation. Vatican II set a new stage in terms of correlation between theology, liturgy and spirituality in a response to the needs of the people as the result of the twentieth century Liturgical Movement. It is an authentic renewal at the same time rooted in the Tradition of the Church. In essence this edition is united with the Roman Rite.

Fifthly this new edition was encouraged by the *Plenaria* in 1991. There was no intention to create altogether a new Missal discarding the old one, but only to bring out a new edition of the post-Vatican II missal with textual and rubrical modifications.

Though these above reasons help us to understand the necessity for the third typical edition, they do not relieve us from the responsibility of understanding the significance of the content of the missal and its implication in pastoral situations. That is why this missal has to be properly understood before it is being put in to use so that it may yield benefits as intended in the revision. Such liturgical catechesis on the new Missal is necessary both for the priests as well as lay faithful. Need for liturgical catechesis of MR 2002 was already foreseen in the *Plenaria* 1996.

3. The General Instruction of the Roman Missal

Parallel to the development of the three editions of the Roman Missal one must consider another important document which is part of the Missal itself, namely The General Instruction of the Roman Missal (GIRM). For many pastors and Christian faithful the publication of a new liturgical book means merely change in the rubrics and some phrases in the prayers. However what underlies the revision of liturgical texts or promulgation of new editions of Missal such as the one we are considering in this book is to bring unity of the content and the rite: *lex orandi, lex credendi*, that is the intimate connection between the law of prayer and the law of belief. In Christian worship, the community is faithful to the Lord's command and adheres to the Christian tradition in transmitting the faith received through the apostles. Hence the liturgical laws are not merely for the sake of discipline, but above all to keep us faithful to the Christian tradition in the dynamism of liturgy as glorification of God and sanctification of man. That is why St. Paul was concerned about the abuses in the Eucharistic assemblies at Corinth and gave instructions to the believers regarding the dignity of Eucharistic gatherings (I Cor 11:17-34). Even during the early period of Christianity (first three centuries) the improvisations of liturgical prayers were not arbitrary, but they were according to the principles transmitted in the tradition through the apostles. We mentioned in the first chapter of this book that during fourth and fifth centuries when there were abuses in the liturgical assemblies and introduction of prayers with erroneous content, the regional synods took up the issue by giving norms to rectify the same and mandated that prayers need prior approval from a competent authority. The compilation of the liturgical prayers in the subsequent centuries (e.g.: Leonine, Gelasian, and Gregorian sacramentaries), the liturgical reform of Pope St. Gregory the Great and later by Pope St. Pius V with promulgation of General Rubrics and Roman Missal are examples of constant guidelines in the Church to help a meaningful celebration of the Sacred Liturgy. The GIRM that we are considering here also comes in this same line of thought with its unique features after the liturgical reform proceeding from the directives of Vatican II.

The General Instruction is entirely different in character from the General Rubrics of the 1570 Missal of Pius V. The aim is no longer a simple description of the rites but a presentation of the celebration in which doctrinal and pastoral considerations take first place and give meaning to rubrical instructions. According to the original meaning of the Latin title, *Institutio generalis Missale Romanum* (IGMR), we are being given an "instruction" inspired by an interpretative intention and a pedagogical purpose. The regulations and interpretations are given according to the authentic tradition of the Church thus serving the pastoral aspiration of the Church which sees itself as being for humankind a "sacrament" of the salvation bestowed by Jesus Christ.

One of the main characteristics of GIRM is revival of the language of liturgy from ritual to symbol. The theological thrust of GIRM is that liturgical rites are performed no longer for the sake of legal satisfaction, but the renewed liturgy after Vatican II requires something more than mere valid performance of the rite. The ritual language is symbolic language. One should not misunderstand that Vatican II has done away with all rubrics. On the contrary, Vatican II offers enhanced understanding of the rubrics by freeing from a static rubricism to dynamic understanding of the symbolic language in correctly observing the rubrics.

Another important characteristic of the GIRM is to offer clarity in the role of bishops, priests, deacons, duly instituted acolytes, lectors and altar servers during the celebration of the Holy Mass. While preserving the traditional teachings of the Church with regard to the sacrificial nature of the Eucharist, the real presence of Christ in the Eucharist, and the ministerial priesthood, the GIRM promotes active participation of the faithful because, the celebration of liturgy fosters the response and participation of the people in the saving act. The celebration should enable the people to relate their life to the mystery celebrated. The gifts of bread and wine representing their entire life, is brought to the altar symbolizing their spiritual sacrifice by virtue of their Baptism and exercise of common priesthood. The priest celebrant offers these gifts at the altar exercising his ministerial priesthood.

3.1. Development of GIRM after Vatican II

The first stages of the post-Conciliar reform of the Mass were marked by Pope Paul VI's apostolic constitution *Missale Romanum* (1969). Simultaneously the first text of GIRM began to be circulated in 1969. When the first text of the new Missal and the GIRM appeared some experts including two cardinals Alfredo Ottaviani and Antonio Bacci were shocked and openly complained that the revised order of the Mass and GIRM appear to break from the Tradition of the Church.[83] This serious concern was quickly addressed by Introduction and clarification of some sections in the GIRM and included in the Missal of 1970. For example, the Introduction tried to address three major sections: witness to unchanged Faith (nos. 2-5), witness to unbroken Tradition (nos. 6-9), and accommodation to modern conditions (nos. 10-15). Besides these changes in the Introduction, the body of the 1969 GIRM was also changed, especially where doubts of deviation from Catholic theology of the Mass were expressed. Hence significant changes were introduced in numbers 7, 48, 55d and 60 of the old GIRM[84] (See nos. 27, 72, 79d, and 93 in GIRM 2002). This first edition of the GIRM in the 1970 Missal was once again revised in 1972 when Paul VI issued two documents concerning the revision of minor orders and norms for the diaconate: *motu proprio Ministeria Quaedam* and *Ad Pascendum*. Through these documents the order of sub-deacon was suppressed and the role of acolyte was expanded. Therefore there was immediate need to eliminate all reference to

---

[83] A. Bugnini, *The Reform of the Liturgy 1948-1975*, 277-301.

[84] Notitae 6 (1970): 169-193.

sub-deacon in the second edition of the GIRM and include new roles of acolytes with regard to cleansing of the chalice and assisting with communion. With the promulgation of the second typical edition (*editio typica altera*) of the Roman Missal in March 27, 1975, there was further need to revise GIRM and bring it as the third edition. In the third edition of the GIRM in 1975 there were better clarifications and the following changes: various ministries such as acolyte and readers were clarified; naming of the bishop / auxiliary bishop in the Eucharistic prayer was explained; some Roman documents that came after 1970 Missal were included in the footnote; some new texts were added; some terminologies were changed, for example the term "celebrant" was changed to "priest" or "priest celebrant."

On 25th January 1983, the revised Code of Canon Law was promulgated. The new Code of Canon Law addresses some topics concerning the celebration of Mass, such as homily, concelebration, the reservation of the Eucharist, the architecture of churches, and the bread and wine used for the Eucharist. Following the promulgation of the new Code, on 12th September 1983 a list of variations was published which introduced several changes in the GIRM where it referred to the topics mentioned in the new Code of Canon Law. In the same year these variations were incorporated in several sections and footnotes of the fourth edition of the GIRM.[85]

After many years of preparation, the publication of an *editio typica tertia* of the *Missale Romanum* was promulgated by Pope John Paul II in the course of the Jubilee Year of our Redemption and was published in 2002. This long-awaited revision includes a new edition of the IGMR. On November 12, 2002, the Latin Church members of the United States Conference of Catholic Bishops approved a translation of the IGMR prepared by the International Commission on English in the Liturgy (ICEL). The translation was confirmed by the Congregation for Divine Worship and Discipline

---

[85] *Notitae* 19 (1983): 540-543.

of the Sacraments on March 17, 2003.[86] This revised GIRM found in MR 2002 is the fifth edition of the GIRM and it possesses a unique role among all the documents on the liturgy. Like its preceding editions, it has been published in order to give life to a dream.

It was the dream of reformers such as St. Hippolytus, St. Gregory, and St. Leo. It was the dream of Popes John XXIII, Paul VI and clearly remained the vision of Pope John Paul II, who called us to "an ever deeper grasp of the liturgy of the Church, celebrated according to the current books and lived above all as a reality in the spiritual order" (*Vicesimus Quintus Annus,* 1988, no. 14). Likewise, this dream is shared by the Bishops, pastors and people across the globe through synods and *Pleneria*. Finally, it is the vision of the Church itself: the dream of God's people joined to Christ in Baptism and made "ever more holy by conscious, active, and fruitful participation in the mystery of the Eucharist" (GIRM 5 & SC 11).

3.2. The Content of GIRM – 5th Edition

At the first glance one would notice increase in the number of paragraphs from 341 to 399. Though the structure remains the same, many subtitles are changed. The content establishes the dignity of Eucharistic celebration in clear terms, clarifies the roles of deacons, and other ministers assisting priest during the liturgy, clarifies the bishop's liturgy in a particular church, and defines interaction with Episcopal conferences. The present edition of the GIRM has nine chapters:

- The Importance and dignity of the Eucharistic celebration.
- The Structure of the Mass, its elements and its parts.
- The Duties and Ministries in the Mass.
- The Different forms of celebrating Mass.
- The Arrangement and furnishing of churches for the celebration of the Eucharist.

---

[86] Prot. N. 2235/02/L.

- The Requisites for the celebration of Mass.
- The Choice of the Mass and its parts.
- Masses and prayers for various circumstances and Masses for the dead.
- Adaptations within the competence of Bishops and Bishops' Conferences.

3.3. Necessity of New GIRM

The third typical edition of the Roman Missal 2002 included the fifth edition of the GIRM for number of reasons. Some examples of the reasons are explained here below. There was necessity for a new GIRM in the light of recent liturgical documents that came after the previous edition. There was a need to correct several inconsistencies in terminologies. In addition, many have pointed out unnecessary elaboration in certain explanations in the light of thirty years of experience after the previous Missal in 1975. For example, some felt the unnecessary lengthy explanation on the prohibition against women entering sanctuary (See 1975 GIRM 70) or the detailed instruction on distributing Communion from the chalice using a tube or spoon (1975 GIRM 248-252).[87] In light of several editorial changes and omissions it was necessary to renumber the paragraphs of GIRM. The new textual changes bring more clarity. For example, while referring to the reverence shown to the altar, the previous edition mentioned "proper reverence" (*debita reverentia*) which is now substituted "profound bow" (*profunda inclinatio*). While referring to ordained ministers the new text now include "sacred" and references to "acolytes" now include "duly instituted" (*rite institutus*) to avoid confusion with altar servers. In the places where the previous text had the term "says" the new text has "sings or says." In some instances the text is rephrased to bring clarity in the rite. For example, in the rite of peace (2002 GIRM, 82, See 1995

---

[87] D. C. Smolarski, *The General Instruction of the Roman Missal 1969-2002: A Commentary* (Collegeville, MN.: The Liturgical Press, 2003), 26.

GIRM 56b) instead of saying that the faithful "offer some sign of mutual charity…" the new text says that the faithful "express some sign of their ecclesial communion and mutual charity for each other before receiving sacramental Communion." The phrase communicates clearly the link between the "ecclesial communion" expressed in the rite of peace and the "sacramental Communion" soon to follow. The final chapter addressing adaptations permitted by the conference of Bishops is new in the 2002 GIRM (nos. 386-399). This chapter in GIRM on adaptations summarizes the principles and procedures found in the 1994 Roman instruction of the Liturgy, the Roman Liturgy and Inculturation (*Varietates Legitimae*). In general the changes in the 2002 GIRM can be seen in four categories: a) some additions do not change existing practice, but merely make explicit what should be done; b) other additions may change present practices in some cases since the previous versions of the GIRM were interpreted in a very broad sense. For example the new GIRM notes that the altar cross is to have the figure of Christ crucified upon it (nos. 117, 308). The 2002 GIRM is very clear that only the Book of the Gospel is carried in procession and not the Lectionary (no. 120d); c) other additions emphasize good liturgical practice. For example, the 2002 GIRM (no. 147, 236) emphasizes that the final doxology after the Eucharistic prayer "through him, with him…" is said only by the priest; d) other changes permit new practices within the celebration of the Mass. For example, a bishop is now permitted to bless the assembly with the Book of the Gospels after the proclamation of the Gospel (2002 GIRM 175), imitating the long-standing practice of the papal Masses and Byzantine Rite; and a few changes actually altar what the current legislation prescribes. For example, omitting the psalm on weekdays when the *Alleluia* is sung is no longer an option (2002 GIRM 63a, See 1975 GIRM 38a).

CHAPTER III

THEOLOGICAL AND THE LITURGICAL SIGNIFICANCE OF THE PARTS OF THE MASS

The whole structure of the Mass is clearly synthesized and brought out beautifully by the *General Instruction of the Roman Missal* (GIRM) in these words.

> The Mass is made up as it were of the Liturgy of the Word and the Liturgy of the Eucharist, two parts so closely connected that they form but one single act of worship. For in the Mass the table of God's Word and of Christ's body is laid for the people of God to receive from it instruction and food. There are also certain rites to open and conclude the celebration (GIRM 28).

The rites are arranged in such a way that the Christian community commemorates the paschal mystery of Christ in a meaningful way and has an opportunity to listen to the Word of God in a systematic and orderly way. The structure has pedagogical and pastoral character. It is pedagogical in the sense that it instructs the participants with God's Word and helps them to understand and celebrate the paschal mystery of Christ. It is pastoral in the sense that it is a public worship of the people of God gathered together as an ecclesial community, in which the glorification of God and the sanctification of the members of the church (SC 10) take place through different signs and symbols. Therefore it is the responsibility of the pastors to lead the faithful for a "full, conscious and active participation" (SC 14) as demanded by the very nature of the Eucharist. One would greatly benefit if one understands the meaning and the purpose of the different liturgical actions in the Mass. The following chart assists to understand various parts of the Mass:

General Structure of the Mass with Individual parts and their meaning

General Structure	Meaning	Individual parts
1.Introductory Rites	Assembling and preparing the community through greetings, penitential rite and prayer.	Entrance hymn/Antiphon, veneration of altar, incensing, greeting and introduction. Penitential rite, *Kyrie* (on Sundays rite of blessing and sprinkling water), *Gloria* and opening prayer.
2. Liturgy of the Word	Proclamation of the Word of God; meditation and response of the assembly.	First reading, Responsorial psalm, Second reading, Acclamation (or sequence) before the gospel, Gospel and homily. Creed and intercessions.
3. Liturgy of the Eucharist	I. Preparation of gifts; prayer of thanks over the bread and wine; act of offering one's self	Procession bringing gifts, prayers of preparation, incensation, washing of hands and prayer over the gifts.
	II. Eucharistic Prayer; thanksgiving for God's saving acts, Transubstantiation.	Preface, *Sanctus*, epiclesis – praying for the power of the Holy Spirit to transform the gifts, institution narrative, acclamation, anamnesis, offering, intercessions and doxology.
4.Communion Rite	Communion, Union with Christ in the Sacred meal.	The Our Father, embolism, acclamation, rite of peace, breaking of bread, commingling, *Agnus Dei*, prayers of preparation, reception of communion, giving thanks and concluding prayer.
5. Concluding Rite	Blessing and Dismissal	Pastoral announcements, blessing, dismissal, kissing of altar and leaving.

We will highlight some theological and liturgical significance of these five parts of the Mass one by one.

1. Introductory Rites

1.1. Preparation for the Mass

"After the people have assembled" (*populo congregato*): these are the first words in the description of the Mass both in the *Order of Mass* (n.1) and GIRM (n.47). It indicates that people with different experience and from every walk of life come to the church with one purpose, the purpose is to worship. It prepares them to participate in the mass both physically and spiritually. That is why it is strongly recommended that people should be instructed and trained to assemble in the church a few minutes before the Eucharistic celebration. It prepares the people to assemble on time and puts them in proper mind setting to begin the liturgy. In the earlier times praying of the psalms, the recitation of the rosary and doing some other pious activities marked the gathering of the people for the Mass. In many churches, especially in the East, canonical hours and certain sections of the office were recited before the Mass as an introduction for the celebration of the Mass.[88] What is important is the "assembling" or coming together of the community and this "assembling" was seen in the first century as a picture of the redeemed Church, which is symbolized by the many grains of wheat that have become one loaf of bread.[89]

1.2. Entrance Hymn & Procession

When the people are assembled the mass begins with the entrance procession and this is accompanied by the entrance song. The entrance hymn is the first action of the celebration and it has a threefold function:

To intensify the unity of the gathered people: "After the people have assembled, the entrance song begins as the priest and the ministers come in" (GIRM 47). The song is not a concert. Its

---

[88] A.G.Martimort, ed., *The Church at Prayer*, vol. 2, 75.

[89] *Didache* 9.

primary intention is to promote communication. The unity of voices expresses a communion among the singers. It should inspire active participation. Hence congregational singing is very much encouraged and role of the choir is to lead the congregation in singing. Otherwise the choir could sing the verse and the congregation join the chorus or antiphon.

To lead their thoughts to the mystery of the season of feast: Music and song create the proper mood and mind setting for the whole celebration. The entrance song should suit the mystery of the liturgical season and degree of festivity. Its theme should be related to the celebration. The purpose of the entrance song is "to open the celebration, intensify the unity of the gathered people, lead their thoughts to the mystery of the season or feast, and accompany the procession of priest and ministers" (GIRM 47). The Missal itself gives a wide variety of entrance antiphons which are taken from psalms or other texts from Scripture. In some cases other appropriate songs which are approved by the local Bishops' conference could be sung.[90]

To accompany the procession: Depending upon the occasion of the liturgical celebration, the entrance procession could take solemn form, but it is always part of the act that establishes the assembly. If the Book of the Gospels is carried by the deacon or reader, it is kept on the altar. The entrance procession normally should start from the entrance of the church and proceed towards the altar.

1.3. Veneration of the Altar

When the priest, the other ministers and servers reach the altar, they make a proper sign of reverence, that is a profound bow or, if there is a tabernacle containing the Blessed Sacrament, a genuflection (GIRM 122). If the cross has been carried in the procession, it is placed near the altar or at some other convenient

---

[90] GIRM 47, See also: DD 55.

place. After the bow, the priest approaches the altar and kisses it. Like the bow or genuflection, the kiss is given to the altar and to Christ himself as represented by the altar. The incensation of the altar is optional (GIRM 49). However on Sundays and solemn celebrations it is encouraged. Thurification or incensation is an expression of reverence and of prayer which is signified in Sacred Scripture (Ps 141 [140]:2, Rev 8:3).

1.4. Greeting and Introduction

After kissing and incensing the altar, the priest takes his place at the presidential chair and leads the remaining introductory rites and the concluding rite. The presidential chair, which is set up opposite and in the sight of the congregation, is an expression of the hierarchic structure of God's people. In the person of his minister, Christ himself presides over the service and the priest represents him (GIRM 310).

Different liturgical actions unfold from its proper place. Liturgical Space plays an important role as different gestures and postures of the congregation. There is a place for the introductory and concluding rites; there is a place for the Liturgy of the Word and a place for the liturgy of the Eucharist. And these places are used only at appropriate occasions during the liturgical celebration. The nature of the Eucharistic celebration demands that these norms are followed accordingly.

Next the priest and the faithful, still standing, make the sign of the cross on themselves. The sign of the cross as an introduction to prayer has a long tradition, which regards the making of the sign on oneself an act of self-blessing before prayer. The sign of the cross also contains a double confession: our salvation is based only on the Cross of Christ and Christ's redeeming death on the cross is to become a sacramental presence in this celebration. The accompanying words are confession of the triune God, the source and goal of our salvation. At the same time, the sign of the cross made in the name of the triune God becomes a way of remembering our baptism. In this name we were born in baptism and made members of the people of God. We have been plunged into the same paschal mystery of the Lord:

> Do you not know that all of us who have been baptized into Christ Jesus were baptized into his death? Therefore we have been buried with him by baptism into death, so that, just as Christ was raised from the dead by the glory of the Father, so we too might walk in newness of life (Rom 6:3-4).

After the sign of the cross, the priest greets the congregation with gesture and word: the gesture of outstretched arms and a wish for blessings. The General Instruction combines a high sense of purpose with this greeting: "Through his greeting the priest declares to the assembled community that the Lord is present. This greeting and the Congregation's response express the mystery of the gathered Church" (GIRM 50). "The purpose of these (introductory) rites is to permit the assembled faithful to establish communion among themselves" (GIRM 46). The congregation's answer is "And with your spirit."[91] Just as the president's greeting is not simply an expression of his personal goodwill and readiness to communicate with the congregation, but it is a proclamation of salvation in the name of Christ, so too the congregation is not responding to an individual person with a human function but to the minister who is a "servant of Christ and steward of the mysteries of God" (1 Cor 4:1).

"The priest, deacon, or other capable minister can say a few words, introducing the faithful to the Mass of the day."[92] This introduction to some extent continues the work of the greeting in as much as it fosters the sense of community in the celebrating congregation and makes it easier to experience the mystery. The

---

[91] For detailed explanation of the response "And with your spirit" see page 104 of this book.

[92] Rubrics in the Roman Missal.

introduction initiates the assembly to the theme of the liturgy; hence brief.

1.5. Penitential Rite

From the beginning the Christians felt the need of purification before taking part in the Eucharist. Thus *Didache*, speaking about Sunday assembly mentions that confession of sins comes first. "Come together on the Lord's Day, break bread and give thanks, having first confessed your sins so that your sacrifice may be pure."[93] The first form of the penitential rite consists of a common confession of sin that is based on the earlier *Confiteor*. We confess our sins not only to "almighty God" but also to all our "brothers and sisters". This makes the social dimension of our failures clear. It consists not only in the fact that we, through our misdeeds, have done injustice to our fellow human beings and have violated love but also in the fact that we have injured the Body of Christ and destroyed what others are working to build up. The *Confiteor* closes with the petition "I ask blessed Mary, ever virgin, all the angels and saints, and you, my brothers and sisters to pray for me to the Lord our God". This confession in one another's presence and the intercession for one another, correspond to the instruction of the Letter of James: "Therefore confess your sins to one another, and pray for one another, so that you may be healed" (5:16).

The second form of the penitential rite consists of a brief prayer prayed in alternation by the priest and the congregation. The third form combines three invocations of Christ together with the three acclamations of the "Lord have mercy" (*kyrie*). When this form is used, the *kyrie* following the absolution is omitted. In all the forms of the penitential rite the priest prays for forgiveness. This prayer said by the priest is not a formula of absolution pronounced at the Sacrament of Reconciliation but it is a petition for pardon.

---

[93] *Didache* 14, in L. Deiss, *Springtime of the Liturgy* (Collegeville, MN: The Liturgical Press, 1967), 77.

The penitential rite may be completely omitted if the Mass is preceded by another liturgical act, such as some part of the Liturgy of the Hours, or in baptismal Mass. Two examples may help to see this happening in parish context: Rite of Blessing and Sprinkling holy water on Sundays especially during Easter season and Blessing of Palms and procession on Palm Sunday are done in the place of penitential rite.

1.6. Rite of Blessing and Sprinkling of Holy Water

In the history of salvation, water has a great significance. God's chosen people had this powerful and soothing experience of divine providence at the waters. In the book of Genesis we read, "The Spirit of God was moving over the face of the waters" (Gen 1:2). God's mighty hand showed its power when His chosen people met a dead end at the Red sea. Yahweh divided the waters of Red sea and made a way for the Israelites to march towards the Promised Land. (Ex 14:16-31) His divine providence provided water from the rock for the thirsty sojourners in the desert (Ex 17:6). When Samaria was hit by severe drought for three years, God sent rain after the prayer by Prophet Elijah (I Kings 18:1-45). Prophet Ezekiel envisioned the new Israel renewed by the spring of living water flowing from the Lord's presence in the temple of Jerusalem (Ezk 47:1-12). In the New Testament we read Jesus received baptism at the waters of Jordan and the Spirit descended upon him and Heavenly Father acknowledged Him as His beloved son (Mt 3:16-17). At Cana the ordinary water was changed into wine, a great source of blessing for the wedding host (Jn 2:1-11). St. Paul in his letters speaks about water as symbol for baptism which is a sharing in the paschal mystery of Jesus Christ. According to Paul, Baptism is dying to sin and rising to new life with Christ. The last book of the Bible, Revelation beautifully explains the symbolism of water as God's blessing. "Then he showed me the river of the water of life, bright as crystal, flowing from the throne of God and of the Lamb through the middle of the street of the city..." (Rev 22:1-5). In the tradition of the Church too, water has been seen as symbol of God's blessing.

Every Sunday as the community gathers to celebrate the paschal mystery in Eucharistic liturgy, it begins with the rite of blessing of water. It reminds us of our experience of the paschal mystery of Jesus through our baptism – dying to sin and rising to new life (Col 2:12; Rom 6:4-6).

In the Christian initiation which took place during the Easter vigil, Baptism, Confirmation and the Eucharist formed one whole, constituting the introduction of the new Christian into the Church. These sacraments were presented immediately succeeding one another. The Eucharist began with the procession, which lead the newly baptized from the baptistery to the Church. This solemn moment was recalled by St. Ambrose in the following words:

> The people who have been purified and enriched with wonderful gifts (Baptism and Confirmation) begin to walk in procession to the altar, saying: 'I will go to the altar of God, to God who rejoices my youth.' Having stripped themselves of the last traces of the ancient error, renewed in the youth of the eagle, they hasten to go to the heavenly banquet. They enter, then, and, seeing the holy altar prepared, they cry out: 'You have prepared a table before me.'[94]

St. Gregory of Nazianzen develops this symbolism of the procession as a figure of the entrance into the heavenly sanctuary, taking his inspiration from the eschatological parable of the wise virgins.

This rite of blessing and sprinkling of holy water in the Roman liturgy indicates the close relationship between the sacraments of Baptism and Eucharist. The introductory prayer for this rite found in the Roman Missal says, "Dear friends, this water will be used to remind us of our Baptism."[95] The prayer used in this rite has

---

[94] J. Danielou, *The Bible and the Liturgy*, (Notre Dame, IN: University of Notre Dame Press, 1956), 129.

[95] Roman Missal 2002, Rite of blessing and sprinkling holy water.

penitential tone. "It washes away our sins and brings us eternal life."[96] That is why GIRM says, "On Sundays, especially in the season of Easter, in place of the customary act of penance, the blessing and sprinkling of water to recall baptism may at times take place" (GIRM 51). During the Easter season, this rite has special prayer for blessing of water. The final prayer in this rite has eschatological tone as expressed by St. Gregory of Nazianzen: "May almighty God cleanse us of our sins, and through the Eucharist we celebrate make us worthy to sit at his table in his heavenly kingdom."[97]

1.7. Gloria

Immediately after the Penitential Rite or the Rite of Blessing and Sprinkling of water, we sing the Gloria. The *Gloria* is clearly intended to create a festive spirit (GIRM 53). The liturgical norm does not permit the use of any other texts other than approved by the competent authorities, because *Gloria* echoes the biblical passage that has theological significance in liturgy. This festive hymn that begins with the words of the gospel (Lk 2:14) when the angels announced the birth of the messiah to the shepherds of Bethlehem reminds us that liturgy is the extension of Incarnation where we celebrate God's presence here and now.

1.8. Opening Prayer

This prayer brings to close the Introductory Rites. This prayer is one of the presidential prayers. This prayer has a three-part structure: invitation to prayer; moment of silence; prayer with Trinitarian conclusion. The invitation is very short: "Let us pray". Although only the priest speaks the prayer, everyone who participates in the celebration becomes "a pray-er" of this prayer.

After the invitation to pray there is a brief moment of silence. The document describes this silence as follows: "They observe a

---

[96] Ibid.

[97] Roman Missal.

brief silence that they may realize they are in God's presence and may call their petitions to mind" (GIRM 54). Silence is part of the structure of the liturgy. The Constitution on the Sacred Liturgy (SC 30) and the GIRM (45) emphasize this point. The GIRM also indicates various functions of the moment of silence: reflection at the confession of guilt and after the invitation to prayer; short meditation after readings and homily; and interior prayer of praise after Communion. Prayer and worship are not activities to be completed as quickly as possible. It is only in quiet that people can become aware of themselves and turn their hearts to God. In this silence, individual worshippers are also able to clarify the identity of the persons and situations they are remembering in prayer.

The prayer that follows was formerly called "collect". This name was derived from the Latin term *oratio collecta*, which means "prayer that has been gathered". The celebrant sums up the prayers of the congregation. In addition, "in it he gives expression to the special character of the celebration" (GIRM 54). The spiritual content of this prayer is very rich. After the address to God and the mention of an attribute that is determinative or at least especially relevant to the feast (omnipotence, eternity, love of men, fatherhood), a sentence names the great deeds of God in the creation and conservation of the world, as well as in revelation and redemption. The reason for now approaching God is his fidelity and the fact that what he has done in the past he will continue to do in the future. That is why all the orations end with "through Christ our Lord".

As in the case with all presidential prayers, the opening prayer is spoken with raised and extended hands. This is called the "stance of the prayer", the posture of the praying figures depicted on the walls in the Roman catacombs. For early Christians, raising the arms and extending the hands during prayer was also a reminder of the posture of the crucified Lord.

The opening prayer ends with the people's response "Amen". This means, "Yes, it is so", or "Yes, so be it". With this, the congregation makes the priest's prayer their own and simultaneously adds their signatures to this document of prayer. In the Mass only one opening prayer is said. Due to logical reason and the very nature of the liturgy, the liturgical norms do not allow combination of two or more opening prayers in the same mass.

2. Liturgy of the Word

2.1. Sacred Scripture and Liturgy

The unity of Scripture and liturgy had long been witnessed by the biblical religion. From the beginning, the two have been united indissolubly. Scripture is for liturgy, and Scripture is about liturgy. Liturgy likewise, proclaims the scriptures even as it interprets and actualizes them. The unity of scripture and liturgy may be described as both material and formal. The unity is material in the sense that the content of Scripture is largely concerned with the liturgy, and the content of the liturgy is drawn from Scripture. Liturgy figures most prominently the key moments in salvation history.[98] That is why Pope Benedict XVI in his Post-Synodal Apostolic Exhortation, *Verbum Domini* says, "the liturgy is the privileged setting in which God speaks to us in the midst of our lives...Every liturgical action is by its very nature steeped in sacred Scripture."[99]

Their relationship is formal in the sense that different books in Scripture took the final form for the sake of liturgy, and the canon itself was derived from liturgical tradition. James A. Sanders made this observation of canonical study: "That which is canon comes to us from ancient communities of faith, not just from individuals ...The whole of the Bible, the sum as well as all its parts, comes to us out of the liturgical and instructional life of early believing communities."[100] William J. Abraham in his book on *Canon* writes

---

[98] S. Hahn, *Letter and Spirit,* (New York: Doubleday, 2005), 33.

[99] Benedict XVI, *Verbum Domini* Post-Synodal Apostolic Exhortation, Vatican 2010, #52.

[100] J. A. Sanders, *From Sacred Story to Sacred Text* (Philadelphia: Fortress, 1987), 162.

that, "The canon of Scripture was simply a list of books to be read in worship and to be used for spiritual direction and instruction in the Church."[101]

2.1.1. In the Old Testament

The Liturgy of the Word that we celebrate today has its roots in the Bible. In the OT, several texts perfectly illustrate the purpose of various rites presently observed in the church. Today, the liturgical assembly is like the *Qahal Yahweh* of the O.T., which gathers together in the first place to hear God speaking to it: "For if only you would listen to him today, 'Do not harden your hearts as at Meribah…'" (Ps 95:7-8). In the later development of Judaism after exile the reading from the scriptures formed essential part of the liturgy at synagogues.

2.1.2. In the New Testament

Christian liturgy inherited from the synagogue the practice of reading at each prayer some passages from the scriptures (Lk 4:16-21, Acts 13:27). However, the Christian liturgy gave a new meaning: the risen Christ on the road to Emmaus explained to them the passages throughout the scriptures that were about himself, before making himself known in the breaking of the bread (Lk 24:27,31). In the same event he explained to the apostles everything written about him in the Law of Moses, the prophets and the psalms must be fulfilled (Lk 24:44). Thus the mutuality between Sacred Scripture and liturgy - a tradition that is continuous from the Old Testament period - found newer and distinct expressions in the proclamation of the early Christian liturgies. The Christological hymns of the New Testament and proclamations like "Jesus is the Lord" (I Cor 12:3, Rom 19:9, Phil 2:11) and "maranatha" (I Cor 16:22, Rev 22:20), are examples of continuous, but distinct early Christian expressions used in the liturgical context as witnessed by the NT writings. The early

---

[101] W. J. Abraham, *Canon and Criterion in Christian Theology* (Oxford: Clarendon Press, 1998), 413.

Christians believed in the fulfillment of the law, prophets and all the OT promises in Christ. The OT promises are viewed from a new Christological perspective.[102]

2.1.3. In the Tradition of the Church

The importance given to the reading from Scripture in Christian liturgy during the apostolic period continued in the subsequent centuries. This practice is acknowledged by Justin Martyr in his *First Apology*, written in 155 AD: "The memories of the apostles and the writings of the prophets are read in so far as time permits."[103] The OT prepared for the understanding of NT, which takes to the future. It is with this dialectic that the Fathers of the Church read the scriptures. For example, *Jerusalem* is not merely a historical city but also the place of the royal messiah and alludes primarily to the Church and then to heavenly Jerusalem in the final fulfillment. Events in Scripture are not merely past events but have relation to the present and to the future. The same dialectics continues in liturgy.[104] The revealed Word of God is enfleshed in the sacred liturgy, a characteristic evident since the apostolic period. The Prayer of the Church has preserved and developed this characteristic in every century and tried to give perfect expression for the same in its formularies rooted in the Tradition.

In the course of time, the importance given to the Sacred Scripture was obscured with various other elements. Nevertheless, liturgical reforms and decrees of various councils in the history of the Church constantly attempted to restore to original vigor. For example, the Council of Trent in its fifth session canon four had already emphasized the importance of opening the treasures of the

---

[102] R. E. Brown, et al., "Aspects of New Testament Thought" in NJBC, 1354-1381. See also SC #7 in Flannery, 120-121; IBC, 124.

[103] Justin, *Apologia I* 67, 3-5. in L. Deiss, *Springtime of Liturgy*, 92-94.

[104] M. D. Chenu, *La Theologie Comme Science* (Paris: Libraire Philosophique, 1957), 15-17.

Word of God to the people during liturgy. It required bishops and priests to preach on all Sundays, holydays, and the entire season of Advent and Lent.[105] *The Catechism of the Council of Trent*, which is often known as the "Roman Catechism", too insisted the same when it described bishops and priests as "the interpreters and heralds of God."[106] However, as Cardinal Joseph Ratzinger (Benedict XVI) observes, "...unfortunately, precisely this [preaching the Word of God] important part of the accomplishments of Trent has practically disappeared from later theological manuals."[107] Vatican II wanted to rectify this lacuna and tried to restore the original importance of the scripture readings and thus opening more generously the treasures of Sacred Scripture.[108] *Sacrosanctum Concilium,* the Vatican II's Constitution on Sacred Liturgy states:

> Sacred scripture is of the greatest importance in the celebration of the liturgy. For it is from it that lessons are read and explained in the homily, and psalms are sung. It is from the scriptures that the prayers, collects, and hymns draw their inspiration and their force, and those actions and signs derive their meaning. Hence, in order to achieve the restoration, progress, and adaptation of the sacred liturgy it is essential to promote that sweet and living love for sacred scripture to which the venerable tradition of Eastern and Western rites gives testimony (SC. 24).

---

[105] Tanner, vol. 2, 664, 667.

[106] *The Catechism of the Council of Trent,* trans. T. A. Buckley (London, 1852), II.7.2 as cited in A. Nichols, *Holy Order: The Apostolic Ministry from the New Testament to the Second Vatican Council* (Lancaster, PA: Veritas Press, 1991), 174.

[107] Ratzinger, *Principles of Catholic Theology*, 265.

[108] For more detailed study on the Bible and Liturgy and specialized study on the Liturgy of the Word see S. Joseph Lionel, *Speak O Lord,* (Bangalore, India: Asian Trading Corporation, 2006)

With this theological and historical background let us now examine formation of Lectionary and arrangement of scripture readings for liturgy.

2.2. Formation of Lectionary

2.2.1. The Only Liturgical Book in the Early Days

In the beginning of Christian history, Bible was the first and only liturgical book. To what Christians inherited from the tradition of synagogue, the early Church added the texts from the teachings of the apostles to which the first Christians remained faithful (Acts 2:42) and above all the very words of Jesus in the gospel. It became a custom throughout the Church that the final reading should be from the gospel as it is the fulfillment of the Law of Moses, psalms and prophets and which sheds its light on the other New Testament writings. The readings began at the point where it was stopped in the previous liturgy and continued until the president of the liturgy gave a signal to stop. This was known as *lectio continua* (continuous reading). The homily explained how these readings were fulfilled in the hearing of the people.

2.2.2. Formation of *Comes*

Once liturgical year began to take shape, the *lectio continua* was interrupted on certain days and made way for passages more apt to the feast being celebrated especially in the context of honor shown to martyrs. In this situation, 'a reading list' or *comes* (companion) was introduced in order to keep a record of the passage from Scripture that were appropriate for various circumstances. In practice, the list took the form of marginal notes in the copy of the Bible used in a particular church or a list placed at the beginning or end of the volume. In such notes, the first and last words of the passage were indicated as guidance. In the Latin speaking countries this list came to be known as *Capitulare*. In the subsequent years, gradually this list developed into lectionaries containing readings required by the liturgical calendar. The lectionaries were broken into several volumes, and one containing the gospels was given special homage and veneration. In the Roman Mass of the seventh century, it was carried to the altar before the entrance of the bishop, and in Constantinople at the same period, "entrance of the gospel signified the coming of the Son of God." This is the first attestation of the "Little entrance" as it was known then.[109] However important the book is in itself, it acquires its full meaning only when it is proclaimed in the sight of all the people, so that they may receive the word of life from it. The readings were taken from the canonical books. The council of Hippo in 393 AD decreed that "apart from the canonical books nothing is to be read in the Church under the name of 'divine scriptures.'"[110] History informs us that in some of the churches in early history of Christianity, they read three, four or even six readings. In the West, the Milanese liturgy, three readings were read. In the east, the Armenian Rite had three readings (prophet, apostle and gospel); the Coptic Rite had four readings (*paulos, catholica, praxis* and gospel) and Syrian Rite had six readings (law, wisdom, prophets, acts, apostle and gospel)[111]

2.3. New Lectionary

2.3.1. Implementation of Reforms of Vatican II

The Second Vatican Council asked that

...the treasures of the Bible are to be opened up more lavishly so that a richer fare may be provided for the faithful at the table of God's Word. In this way a more representative part of the sacred scriptures will be read to the people in the course of a prescribed number of years (SC 51).

---

[109] St.Germanus of Constantinople, *Exegesis* 24, in N.Borgia, *Il commentario liturgico di S.Germano patriarca constantinopolitano e la versione Latina di Anastasio Bibliotecario* (Grottaferrata, 1912), 21.

[110] *Breviarium Hipponense* 36, ed. C. Munier, *Concilia Africae* (CCL 149; Turnhout: Brepols, 1974), 43.

[111] A. Raes. *Introductio in Liturgiam orientalem* (Rome: Instituto Orientale, 1947), 76-79.

The Consilium entrusted with the task of implementing the directions of Vatican II in the liturgical reform began the work immediately. The official edition of the new Lectionary appeared on May 25, 1969 and from November 30, on the first Sunday of Advent it came into effect. The oldest Lectionary of the Roman Church, containing Epistles and Gospels, dates from the seventh century. Thus the new Lectionary replaced a book, which had served the Church for twelve centuries.

2.3.2. Principle of *Lectio Continua*

The Church wants to give an opportunity that all the books of the Bible could be read in the liturgy. Hence, the practice of continuous reading (*lectio continua*) to understand the mystery of salvation was organized. This method was already used in synagogues and in early Christian liturgies. At Mass the *lectio continua* generally distributed both the cycle of the gospel readings and the cycle of readings of the other parts of the Bible over a whole year. The practice of continuous reading was arranged in such a way that certain books of the Bible were assigned to a particular period of the year, thus giving it a special character. For example during the paschal season the readings from the Acts of the Apostles and the Gospel according to John are read in the Mass. During advent the readings from prophet Isaiah is read since it has messianic prophecies. In principle, the liturgy gives the text of a passage in its entirety, without abridgement or modification. However, there are a few exceptions to this strict rule: the beginning and ending of the reading may have initial or concluding formulas such as: "Jesus said to crowds and to his disciples," "Jesus spoke to the chief priests and elders of the people in parables saying," and "As Jesus and his disciples gathered in Galilee, Jesus said to them." Rarely some intermediary verses are suppressed with a view of stressing the closeness to certain texts to one another or underlining some particular aspect.

2.3.3. Source of Interior Renewal

Vatican II has repeatedly stressed that reading of the Holy Scripture is the chief source of interior renewal for God's people.

Therefore the council decreed, "In sacred celebrations a more ample, more varied, and more suitable reading from sacred scripture should be restored" (SC 35/1). In the readings from Scripture, which are explained in the homily, "God himself speaks to his people; he unfolds to them the mystery of salvation and nourishes their spirit; Christ is present amidst the faithful" (GIRM 55). Hence, the lectionary provides texts for Sundays, feast days and weekdays throughout the year and also for the memorial days of the saints and other special occasions. The arrangement of the readings in the lectionary provides the faithful an opportunity to listen to most important scriptural texts within a reasonably brief space of time.

2.4. Lectionary: Some General Principles

2.4.1. What is Lectionary?

Lectionary is the book that contains the readings from the Sacred Scripture to be used in the Christian Liturgy and these readings are arranged in a systematic way according to the liturgical year. For Sundays there are three readings, the first from the Old Testament and second from the writings of apostle and third reading from the gospel. The purpose of these three readings is to show the unity of the OT and NT and the continuity in the history of salvation. There are three cycles for the readings used on Sundays and they are designated as: A,B,C. There are two principles that govern the choice of readings for Sundays:

- for the Sundays of the Advent, Lent and Eastertide, the readings of the OT and the Apostle are centered around the theme of the gospel, which is known as 'thematic principle.'
- for the other 33 Sundays during the year, the gospel and the second reading are semi-continuous and independent from one another.

For the weekdays during Lent the two readings bear the character of this season. It is time of penance and of preparation for baptism. The two readings of Advent and Eastertide are chosen according to the theme of the liturgical season.

2.4.2. Lectionary for Ordinary Time

The Sundays and weekdays of ordinary time acquire their liturgical and theological themes from the readings assigned to these Sundays in the Lectionary. In the choice of readings, the principle of *semi-continuous* reading is followed. That is, a book of the Bible is read through, although for pastoral reasons certain parts are omitted. One should not be too quick to omit certain verses but it should be done without affecting the style, purpose and meaning of the scriptural passage.

2.4.3. Sundays in Ordinary Time

For the Sundays of Ordinary Time, OT readings are chosen with the theme of the gospel in mind. The aim is to prevent introduction of too many themes and to bring out the unity of OT and NT. It also keeps in mind that the people know OT texts highlighting more important moments in the history of salvation. The NT readings are from the letters of Paul and James. The letters of Peter and John are read during Easter and Christmas seasons. The gospel passages are taken from Mathew in Year A, Mark in Year B, and Luke in Year C. However, there is an exception. On the 2nd Sunday of Ordinary time, three passages from John are chosen that echo the feast of Epiphany and Sundays 17-21 in Year B on which the 6th chapter of John, the discourse of "bread of life" is used. On the 34th Sunday, the last Sunday of Ordinary time when we celebrate the feast of Christ the King, OT reading is about Christ the King prefigured by David and proclaimed in the humiliation he suffered by dying for us on the cross, who governs and guides his church until his return at the end of time.

2.4.4. Weekdays of Ordinary Time

During the Ordinary Time, gospel is the same every year. There are two annual cycles for the non-gospel reading from Scripture with series I for the odd numbered years and series II for the even numbered years. The first reading alternates every few weeks between the OT and NT depending on the length of the book being read. The history of salvation up to the Incarnation of Christ is an important criterion for selection of readings. Only a few books of the OT could not be included in the weekly lectionary such as Prophets Obadiah and Zephaniah and the Song of Solomon, the books of Esther and Judith. Nonetheless, these books are represented on some days in the Advent and Easter seasons. The gospel passages are from the three synoptic gospels in the form of *semi-continuous* reading of the texts. In weeks 1-9 they are from Mark, 10-21 from Mathew and 22-34 from Luke. If the memorial of a saint or mass for a special occasion is chosen, the celebrant tries to assure continuity in the weekday readings. Generally, for such special masses the weekly readings are not changed unless that celebration has some special emphasis or importance to the community that celebrates the liturgy.[112] When a saint's name is mentioned in the scriptural readings, that reading is to be preferred. For example, Mary Magdalene, Timothy, Titus, Barnabas, etc. Thus as Pope Benedict XVI acknowledges in his Apostolic Exhortation, *Verbum Domini* that the revised Lectionary after Vatican II has given us a richer access to Sacred Scripture in the liturgy.[113]

2.5. Elements in the Liturgy of the Word

2.5.1. First Reading

The first reading is taken from the OT, except during the Easter season, when it is taken from the Acts of the Apostles, and corresponds to the gospel reading for the day. The thematic correspondence of OT readings to the gospel of the Mass may consist in the one of the following: promise and fulfillment of OT parallels to the persons and events described in the gospel; thematic

---

[112] A. Adam, *The Liturgical Year,* (New York: Pueblo Publishing Company, 1981).

[113] *Verbum Domini,* 2010, #57.

parallels, for example, the prophets' call to repentance and similar call by Jesus or his forerunner; and the calling of the prophets and that of the apostles.

2.5.2. Responsorial Psalm

The first reading is followed by the Responsorial Psalm. It has the function of marking the end of what has been heard and providing space for meditation. The GIRM describes it as "an integral part of the Liturgy of the Word" (n.61). God speaks to the people by doing marvels for them and people respond by celebrating those marvels (Ex 15 and 21, I Sam 2:5, Tob 13:11). This is precisely the ministerial function of the Responsorial Psalm in the liturgy. Due to its function and integral ties with the readings, the responsorial psalm cannot be substituted with any other devotional song. That is why the Instruction *Redemptionis Sacramentum* calls this replacement as "illicit" (RS 62).

2.5.3. Second Reading

On Sundays and on Solemnities, there is a second reading. The second reading is taken from one of the NT writings. This reading forms an integral part of the liturgy and corresponds to the theme of the liturgy for the day or occasion. That is why the Instruction insisted that, "It is also illicit to omit or to substitute the prescribed biblical readings on one's own initiative and especially to substitute other, non-biblical texts for the readings" (RS 62).

2.5.4. Acclamation before the Gospel

The second reading is followed by the acclamation before the Gospel. Unlike the Responsorial Psalm, this acclamation is not a meditative response to a text that has been read but rather a preparation for the Gospel. It is an acclamation of Christ, who will be present in the Gospel. Except during the Lent, it consists of the Alleluia with its corresponding verse. Alleluia is a Hebrew word meaning "Praise Yahweh" and originated in Jewish worship. In all Christian liturgical rites, it is addressed to the risen Lord, corresponding to Revelation 19:1-7. The verse that is framed by Alleluia is frequently taken from the gospel reading of the day. In accordance with the character of Alleluia, the whole congregation must preferably sing it (GIRM 63c). During the singing, all stand and this posture expresses the congregation's reverence for, and their readiness to receive, the One who is coming.

2.5.5. Gospel

The word "Gospel" means "good news". The proclamation of the Gospel is considered the summit of the celebration of the Liturgy of the Word. The General Introduction to the Lectionary for Mass offers the following description: "The reading of the Gospel is the highpoint of the Liturgy of the Word. For this the other readings, in their established sequence from the OT to the NT, prepare the assembly" (n.13). History informs us that from the fifth century, Christian veneration surrounded with honor the book which contained the Gospels. Some were written in gold on parchment of gold. The Missal provides for the placement of the Gospel Book on the altar either at the beginning of the Mass or before the proclamation of the Gospel (GIRM 173). General Instruction declares: "Greater veneration must be given to the reading of the Gospel" (GIRM 60). And this veneration is the one that is given to Christ.

2.5.6. Homily

In its simplest form, the homily is the translation and explanation of the Word of God. The most typical example of such explanation was one given by Ezra, priest and scribe, to the people who were returning from Babylonian captivity around the year 400 BC on the occasion of a solemn celebration of the Law at the Feast of Tents in Jerusalem (Neh 8:1-8). In its highest form, the homily is the actualization of God's Word on the level of the celebrating community. The most typical example is the homily of Jesus at the synagogue of Nazareth. After reading from the Book of Isaiah, Jesus begins his homily with these words: "Today is fulfilled this word that you have just heard" (Lk 4:21). In spite of the four centuries that separate them, these two homilies are joined in the sense that the goal of the homily will always be to translate the Word of God by showing its actuality. Historically, the homily is one of the earliest elements of the Liturgy of the Word. Originally, the homily was a special privilege of the bishop; today, however it is normally given by the priest presiding at the celebration or by the assisting deacon. Vatican II emphasized that it is a part of the liturgy and may not be omitted, especially during the Masses on Sundays and holy days of obligation (SC 52).[114] The homily "is necessary for the nurturing of the Christian life" (GIRM 65). Homily is intended to let the Word of God be heard in the words of human beings, to translate it in a convincing way into language that the hearers can understand, to demonstrate its power to clarify contemporary problems, and to make a summons, and a claim that is understandable. In *Verbum Domini*, Pope Benedict XVI once again draws our attention to the importance of homily. He says,

> The homily is part of the liturgical action and is meant to foster a deeper understanding of the word of God, so that it can bear fruit in the lives of the faithful. ... Generic and abstract homilies which obscure the directness of God's word should be avoided, as well as useless digressions which risk drawing greater attention to the preacher than to the heart of the Gospel message.[115]

As far as the content and form of the homily are concerned, there are various possibilities: homily as an explanation of Scripture, an explanation of the Mass, and mystagogy (explanation of mysteries).

2.5.7. Profession of Faith

The profession of faith, "is to express the assent and response of the people to the scripture reading and homily they have just

---

[114] See also Code of Canon Law 1983, Canons: 756-780

[115] *Verbum Domini*, #59.

heard, and to recall to them the main truths of the faith, before they begin to celebrate the Eucharist" (GIRM 67). The biblical readings and the homily have made us hear God's Word. Now the congregation is summoned to respond to them with a clear "yes" expressed both in their profession of faith and in their faithful lives (James 1:27). They do this explicitly in their common confession of faith. It is an extended "Amen" to the Liturgy of the Word. It is a time for the people to recall the teachings of the faith before they begin to celebrate the Eucharist. On Sundays and other solemnities, the Profession of Faith is said by the priest and people together (GIRM 68). Either the Nicene Creed or Apostles creed can be used. The Creed reminds us of our baptism and thereby summons the congregation to renew their baptism. At the same time this shows the close relationship between Baptism and Eucharist. As part of the Liturgy of the Word, the Creed also praises God who works our salvation. It does so without using words that explicitly praise and glorify God. It is like a hymn proclaiming the great acts of the triune God.

2.5.8. General Intercessions

The Liturgy of the Word concludes with the Universal Prayer or the Prayer of the Faithful. General Intercession is one of the elements of the liturgy that the Constitution on the Sacred Liturgy refers to when it says: "Other parts which suffered loss through accidents of history are to be restored to the vigor they had in the days of the holy Fathers" (SC 50). These prayers had been lost to the rite of the Mass for almost fifteen hundred years. They were preserved only in the solemn orations used on Good Friday. Now the congregation once again makes intercession for all of humanity, for all needs of the Church and the world. In this part people exercise their priestly function by interceding for all humankind. It is appropriate that this prayer be included in all masses celebrated with a congregation so that intercessions may be made for the Church, for civil authorities and for various other needs (GIRM 69). Such intercession breaks through the narrow horizon of egocentricity and awakens our responsibility for the great concerns of humanity and the whole Church. In doing so, the congregation explicitly participates in the common priesthood received in Baptism. With Christ and in Him, the gathered community intercedes for all humanity and thereby realizes the admonition of the first letter to Timothy (I Tim 2:4). The Christian faith understands such prayer for others to be especially effective when it is said as a prayer of the community, because Christ is then united to; and in solidarity with those praying (Mt 18:19-20). The official guidelines for the formulation of intercessions provide that the priest speak the introductory invitation to prayer and the concluding prayer. The intentions of the prayers should normally be announced by the deacon, the cantor, or one or more members of the congregation. The assembly itself accompanies these petitions with responses or silent prayer. In the latter case, enough time must be provided for such silent prayer. As a rule, the sequence of the intentions is to be: for the needs of the Church, for public authorities and the salvation of the world, for those oppressed by any need, for the local community. In particular, celebrations, such as confirmations, marriages, funerals etc., the series of intercessions may refer more specifically to the occasion to make the liturgy more meaningful to the participants (GIRM 70). One should keep in mind that the intercessions should not be too long and restricted to a few may be five or six are ideal.

3. Preparation of the Gifts

The preparation of the gifts is the beginning of the Liturgy of the Eucharist. The purpose of this part of the Liturgy is to do what Christ did at the Supper: "He took bread…the cup." The bringing of the material of sacrifice to the altar has always been the most meaningful way of expressing this intention. The new Missal has restored this rite to its proper place.

3.1. Historical Background

3.1.1. Accounts of St. Justin

St. Justin gives two descriptions on this subject and both are brief. First, in his account on Eucharist, he says that after prayer and kiss of peace, bread and cup of wine diluted with water are carried to the president of the brethren.[116] Secondly, when he talks about Sunday assembly he mentions the homily and goes on to say, "Then we all rise together and pray, and as we have already said, when our prayer is ended, bread and wine, and water are brought in."[117] He adds further, "Those who have plenty and who want to give are free to contribute whatever they wish and whatever is collected is placed near the president and he [uses it] to assist the orphans and widows...he is concerned with helping all those who are in need."

3.1.2. Accounts of Hippolytus

At the beginning of third century, Hippolytus in *Apostolic Tradition,* also speaks twice about bringing of gifts at Mass. After describing the Episcopal consecration he continues: "Let the deacons present the oblation to him and let the bishop, imposing his hands on it, together with the entire college of priests, recite this thanksgiving ..."[118] In another instance he writes about deacon presenting the oblation to the Bishop.

3.1.3. Gifts by the Faithful

It was only natural, in that time which was completely agrarian society that the faithful should provide the matter for consecration: bread and wine represented the essential elements on which the economy was built. St. Cyprian told a wealthy woman: "You should

---

[116] *First Apology* 65: L. Pautigny, ed., *Textes et Documents* 1 (Paris: Picard, 1904), 138-139. See also PG 6, 428.

[117] Ibid., 67; Pautigny ed,142-143. See also PG 6, 429.

[118] *Apostolic Tradition*; B. Botte 1st ed (sc 11), 30; 2nd ed (LQF 39), 10-11.

blush to come to the *dominicum* without a 'sacrifice' and to take [in communion] a part of the 'sacrifice' offered by some poor person."[119] It was a widespread practice in both East and West that people brought the gifts when they came to celebrate Sunday liturgy (*dominicum*).[120]

3.1.4. Offering in the East and Gaul

In the East and in Gaul the offering was made before the beginning of Mass, in the sacristy (*sacrarium*), which is made clear by St. Gregory of Tours. Therefore, the procession was from sacristy to the altar. The gifts were called *mysterium dominici corporis* and contained in tower shaped vessels. This practice was abandoned during the Carolingian era and the Roman liturgy was adopted.

3.1.5. Offering in Africa, Milan, Rome and Spain

The faithful instead of leaving their gifts in the sacristy, before the mass, formed into a procession at the moment of Eucharistic action, to carry the bread and wine into the sanctuary. St. Augustine says that it was accompanied by singing of psalms. There are similar evidence to say that such procession was in practice both in Milan and Rome.[121]

3.2. Significance of the Offering

3.2.1. General Significance

The offering of gifts by the faithful had significance whether it took place at the sacristy before the liturgy or during the liturgy at the entrance to the sanctuary. From the beginning only baptized Christians were allowed to bring the gifts and pagans, heretics and catechumens were not allowed to bring the gifts. This is evident

---

[119] *De opere et eleemosynis* 15; G. Hartel ed (CSEL 3), 384 (PL 4, col 612-613). Here "sacrifice" has the general meaning of fraternal charity, as with St. Irenaeus.

[120] A. G. Martimort, ed., *The Church at Prayer*, vol. 2, 116.

[121] Ibid.

both from Hippolytus and the decision of the Council of Elvira in 305 AD. It is rightly linked to the priesthood of the faithful, who cannot of course consecrate, but who can offer with the hierarchy this unique sacrifice. They symbolically express their active role in this mystical offering through the carrying of the gifts, which are to be consecrated.

3.2.2. Meaning of Offertory Procession

The institution of the offertory procession was chiefly designed to ensure that the offering of the bread and wine by the faithful should appear inseparable from its final, sacrificial destination and prelude to the communion. The faithful approach the altar to present the celebrant with the bread and wine; the celebrant pronounces over them the words of consecration; the laity then return to the altar to receive the gifts which have been consecrated. St. Augustine says, "Just as the priest receives from us that which he offers up for you, so our Priest [Jesus Christ] receives from us that which offers up for us; the flesh in which He was sacrificed."[122]

3.2.3. Preparation of the Gifts

A brief historical survey informs that this part of the Mass, though retaining the basic elements, such as bringing of bread and wine with water and placing them on the altar, had undergone many changes. From a simple action of bringing of bread and wine with water in antiquity, the faithful gradually included contributions for the support of the clergy, the poor and also the church building. In many parts of the Church this became a procession bringing the gifts and was known as the "offertory procession." In early Middle ages, these gifts were considered almost cultic sacrifices. In many parts of the Church the procession with the gifts was also called a sacrificial procession. This led to the development of many prayers and ceremonies and these prayers gave the impression that we were

---

[122] *Enarrationes in Psalmos* 129, 7; cc 40, p.185 (PL 37, col 1700-1701); cf. *Epist.* 111, 8 (PL 33, col. 426-427).

already at this point in the Mass dealing with the transformed gifts. Because of these developments, this part of the Mass was called "Offertory Rite" until the liturgical reform of Vatican II. Henceforth it is no longer known as *Offertory* but it is known as *Preparation of the gifts.*

3.3. Preparation of the Altar

3.3.1. Altar

Altar takes an important place in the liturgy of the Eucharist. It is desirable to have a fixed altar in every church, because it clearly and permanently represents Christ Jesus, the Living Stone (I Peter 2:4, Eph 2:20) (see also GIRM 298). The GIRM gives directions with regard to fixing an altar and decorations around the altar (GIRM 303-308). The altar should be of natural stone but any solid material skillfully constructed may be used with the approval of the conference of Bishops. The altar should be consecrated. In places where Eucharist is not regularly celebrated, a suitable table may be used but always with a clean altar cloth on it. As regards the adornment of the altar the GIRM says that the altar should be covered with at least one cloth. Its shape and size and adornment should be in keeping with the structure of the altar and its dignity. Candles are required during liturgical services to express devotion and festivity. They could be either kept on the altar or around it. Flowers may not be placed on the altar but they are to be kept around the altar either in front or by the side depending upon the available space in the sanctuary.

3.3.2. Preparation

GIRM presents the preparation of the altar in these words: "First the altar, the Lord's table is prepared as the center of the Eucharistic liturgy. The corporal, purificator, chalice, and missal are placed on it. Sufficient hosts (and wine) for the communion of the concelebrants and faithful are to be kept in ciboria and chalice. As far as possible, fresh hosts are to be consecrated in each Mass according to the possible number of attendance. Only in case of unforeseen situations the consecrated hosts kept in the tabernacle are to be used. It is not advisable to keep too many consecrated hosts in the tabernacle. Once the altar is prepared, then the offerings are brought forward. It is desirable for the faithful to present the bread and wine which are accepted by the Bishop, priests or deacon at the suitable place in front of the altar (GIRM 73). From the document it is more than clear that it is at this moment that things needed for the Eucharistic liturgy are brought and placed on the altar. In other words, the altar should be empty till this particular moment.

3.3.3. Procession

One of the three processions restored by the Council is the "Offertory procession" as a continuation of the ancient custom when people brought bread and wine for the liturgy from their homes. The new Missal states: "It is desirable for the faithful to present the bread and wine which are accepted by the priest or deacon at a convenient place" (GIRM 73). This spiritual meaning consists in the fact that the faithful intend to offer themselves together with their gifts in the Eucharistic celebration. They offer their entire lives with joys and sorrows, press and stress of their lives. As the gifts of bread and wine are going to be transformed into His body and blood, the believers pray that their lives are transformed by the grace of God through participating in this sacrament. This inner devotion is also symbolized if, in addition to bread and wine, charitable gifts are brought, such as the usual collections. These material contributions are really an expression of helping love and of responsibility towards the world and the Church. Through this gesture the participation of the faithful in the liturgy of the Eucharist is also expressed. The baskets used in the collections and other contributions are "to be put in a suitable place but not on the altar" (GIRM 73).

3.4. Blessing Formulas

The priest standing at the altar takes the paten with bread and holding it slightly raised above the altar says the prayer "Blessed are you, Lord, God of all creation…", then takes the chalice in the same way, and says the prayer as prescribed in the missal. If there is no offertory song these prayers are said in an audible voice. These two prayers which are revised after Vatican II are to be said one after another and not together. Vatican II instructed:

> The rite of the Mass is to be revised in such a way that the intrinsic nature and purpose of its several parts, as well as the connection between them, may be more clearly manifested, and that devout and active participation by the faithful may be more easily achieved (SC 50).

Following this direction the members of the study group working on the reform of the Mass thought it necessary to replace the prayers of preparation previously used with more suitable prayers. Numerous formulations were considered in this process. Finally they agreed on a text that is modeled after the Jewish prayers of thanksgiving (*Berakoth*).

These prayers said separately holding bread first and then wine, begin with praise of the Creator. For many millennia, bread has been the basic nourishment of peoples. It makes life possible. Thus the gift of bread reminds us of God as creator, preserver, and friend of life. The same is true of the wine, which ancient Israel considered to be a means of nourishment and of salvation, as well as a means of enjoyment. These prayers of blessing refer not only to the Creator but also to the people whose difficult labors have planted the grain and the vines, harvested and processed their fruits, so that they have become nourishment for us. They also become symbols of the human beings themselves who bring these gifts as an offering to God. These prayers close with a reference to their ultimate purpose: they are to become the "bread of life" and "our spiritual drink".

3.5. Other Ceremonies

Before the priest raises the chalice during the prayer of blessing, he pours a little water into the wine.[123] This rite has its roots, first of

---

[123] See Canon 924 and commentary. J. A. Coriden, T. Green and D. Heintschel, ed., *The Code of Canon Law — A Text and Commentary*, (Bangalore: TPI, 1986), 657.

all, in the custom of the classical world of not drinking wine that had not been mixed with water. Jesus quite probably followed this custom at the Last Supper. Beyond this, Christian tradition has seen various symbols in this action. The wine is a symbol of the divinity, and the water a symbol of humanity, while the mingling of the two symbolizes the Incarnation of God in Christ and man's participation in the divinity of the Redeemer which is expressed in the prayer itself: "By the mystery of this water and wine may we come to share in the divinity of Christ, who humbled himself to share in our humanity."

Two short prayers for purification emphasize the preparatory character of this part of the Mass. After the bread and wine have been prepared, the priest bows and says quietly: "Lord God, we ask you to receive us and be pleased with the sacrifice we offer you with humble and contrite hearts." After this prayer, the gifts, the altar, the cross, the priest and the people may be incensed. The prayers that formerly accompanied this action are no longer used. Then the priest washes his hands an action that is also to be seen as part of the inner preparation of the priest. Undoubtedly this was done for practical reasons in earlier times, when the priest accepted gifts in their natural forms. Today, however, it has an exclusively symbolic character. The accompanying prayer expresses this clearly: "Lord wash away my iniquity; cleanse me from my sin."

3.6. Prayer Over the Gifts

The preparation of the gifts ends with the Prayer Over the Gifts and this marks the end of the preparation and of the first part of the Liturgy of the Eucharist. This prayer sums up the content and meaning of the action and provides a transition to the Eucharistic prayer. Beginning in the 8th century in Gallic and French territories, this prayer was spoken softly and as a result became known as the "secret." The Latin *oratio secreta* means "a prayer spoken in a low voice." This prayer being one of the presidential prayers has the same structural pattern as that of the other presidential prayers like the Opening Prayer and Prayer after Communion. Though the other two prayers have a shorter form of invitation "Let us pray" this prayer retains the traditional form existing in the Roman Missal for so many centuries: "Pray brethren, that our sacrifice may be acceptable to God, the almighty Father." Unlike the other two prayers in which the people remain silent, an invitation to pray at this moment is responded to by the congregation.

4. Eucharistic Prayer

Among several splendid prayers in our liturgy such as collects and solemn prayers, the Eucharistic prayers receive the pride of place both by reason of their function and content. In Eucharistic prayer the whole ceremony comes to a climax. Above all it is a priestly prayer, addressed to God the Father through Jesus Christ in the name of all the community. The priest celebrant begins with a dialogue between himself and the people, whom he invites to lift up their hearts to the Lord in thanksgiving and whom he brings into the prayer and the offering of the sacrifice. Hence one must understand that the Eucharistic prayer is a prayer of thanksgiving and sanctification. The Eucharistic prayer is more than just a prayer, but it is the verbal element in the central action of the Mass, because in the Eucharist we are celebrating the sacrifice of the New Law according to the manner which Christ showed us at the Last Supper. That is why the GIRM (n.78) says that it is the center and highpoint of the entire celebration. The meaning of this prayer is that the whole congregation joins Christ in acknowledging the works of God and in offering the sacrifice. This ritual comprises both word and action. We must bear in mind that in the Mass we are not simply reciting some prayer however splendid they are but we are engaged in that which the liturgy itself calls "the work of our redemption."

4.1. Elements of Eucharistic Prayer

The General Instruction of Roman Missal enumerates the chief elements of the Eucharistic prayer as follows: (GIRM 79)

Thanksgiving: The priest praises the Father and thanks Him for the work of salvation or for some special aspect of it in keeping with the day, feast or season. This thanksgiving is expressed especially in the preface. The priest does it in the name of the entire congregation and the congregation responds in the introductory dialogue of preface.

Acclamation: This acclamation, having the semblance of the hymn of heavenly host in the vision of the Prophet Isaiah (Is 6:3), reminds us that we are going to have the same kind of experience of being in the presence of the Lord in the Eucharist. United with the angels, the congregation sings or recites the *Sanctus*. This forms part of the Eucharistic prayer and this hymn should preferably be sung expressing real joy of the theophany.

Epiclesis: The Church makes a special invocation and calls on God's power and asks that the gifts offered by men may be consecrated so that it may become body and blood of Christ and that the victim may become a source of salvation for those who are to share in communion. The invocation of the Holy Spirit to sanctify the offering has been one of the ancient elements in the Eucharistic prayer.

Institution Narrative and Consecration: In the words and actions of Christ, that the sacrifice is celebrated, which he himself instituted at the Last Supper, when, under the appearances of bread and wine, he offered his body and blood, gave them to his apostles to eat and drink, then commanded that they carry on this mystery.

Anamnesis: In fulfillment of the command received from Christ through the apostles, the Church keeps his memorial by recalling especially his passion, resurrection, and ascension.

Offering: In this memorial, the Church, and in particular the Church here and now assembled, offers the spotless victim to the Father in the Holy Spirit. The Church's intention is that the faithful not only offer this victim but also learn to offer themselves and to surrender themselves, through Christ the Mediator, to an ever more complete union with the Father and with each other, so that at last God may be all in all.

Intercession: The intercessions make it clear that the Eucharist is celebrated in communion with the entire Church of heaven and earth and that the offering is made for the Church and all its members, living and dead, who are called to share in the salvation and redemption purchased by Christ's body and blood.

Final Doxology: The praise of God is expressed in the doxology, to which the people's acclamation "Amen" is an assent and a conclusion. The structure of this prayer is such that first the priest pronounces the doxology and people respond with "Amen."

4.2. Preface

.   The word *preface* comes from the Latin word *præ-fari*, which means, "to speak before" or "in the presence of."[124] Specifically in the liturgical context, it means *speaking in the presence of God*[125] before whom we stand to thank and praise.[126] That is why it is an integral part

---

[124] D. Grabner, "Preface," *The New Catholic Encyclopedia*, vol. 11 (New York: Mc Graw Hill Book Company, 1967), 725-727. E. Moeller introduces "preface" as public pronouncement of consecratory prayer based on the meaning of *præfari* in classical Latin. He defines it as proclamation or confession of wonderful deeds of God in creation and salvation. Cf. E. Moeller, *Corpus Præfationum*, x-xxxiv. However, in some ancient sacramentaries we can see few intercessory, doctrinal and catechetical prefaces as well as texts that are panegyrics of saints. Cf. P. Bruylants, "Les préfaces du Missel Romain," LMD 87 (1966): 114-117. The new missal after Vatican II uses the best prefaces from the tradition to return to the original sense of preface as confession of the aspects of the *mirabilia Dei*.

[125] C. Mohrmman, "Sur l'histoire de præfari-Præfatio," VC 7 (1953): 1-2.

[126] L. Bouyer, "La Preface et le Sanctus," LMD 87 (1966): 96. See also L. Soubigou, *A Commentary on the Prefaces and the Eucharistic Prayers of the Roman Missal,* trans. J. A. Otto (Collegeville, MN.: The Liturgical Press, 1971), 3.

of the Eucharistic prayer, the Church's great prayer of thanksgiving.[127] The understanding of preface and canon as different prayers was recognized in the medieval period.[128] GIRM articulates this ancient understanding by acknowledging it among the elements of the Eucharistic prayer.[129]

4.2.1. The Earliest Evidences of the Use of the Term "Preface"

We find the earliest evidence of the present preface-like structure in the *Apostolic Tradition*.[130] In the liturgy that some attribute to Hippolytus, the dialogue introduces the prayer.[131] Preface

---

[127] E. Mazza, *The Eucharistic Prayers of the Roman Rite*, trans. M. J. O'Connell (New York: Pueblo Publications Company, 1986), 36. See also J. Jungmann, vol. 2, 106-107, 115. GIRM includes preface among the elements of Eucharistic prayer. Cf. GIRM #78-79 in LDS II, 40.

[128] In Gregorian Sacramentary, *Præfationes* appears as title for *Vere dignum*. Cf. E. Mazza, *The Eucharistic Prayers of the Roman Rite,* 38.

While J. Jungmann stresses the unity of the entire Eucharistic prayer referred to by the term *Præfatio*, B. Capelle and C. Mohrmann highlight the variation in the use of the term *Præfatio* in the Christian history. In Rome, it may have referred to the Eucharistic prayer and in Gaul it may have referred to admonition before consecratory prayer. Cf. M. G Witczak, *The Language of Eucharistic Sacrifice: Immolare and immolation in prefaces of the Roman Tradition* (Roma: Ponificium Athenæum Anselmianum, 1987), 7.

[129] GIRM mentions that the Eucharistic prayer is the climax of the liturgy and includes prefaces among the elements of this priestly prayer of thanksgiving and sanctification. Cf. GIRM #78,79 in LDS II, 40.

[130] The *Apostolic Tradition* is generally attributed to Hippolytus of Rome (c.215). Hippolytus is considered to be the disciple of Irenaeus. Cf. T. Klauser, *A Short History of the Western Liturgy*, 11. See also P. F. Bradhaw, ed., *The Apostolic Tradition*, 1-5.

[131] B. Botte, *La Tradition apostolique de Saint Hippolyte,* LQF 39 (Münster: Aschendorffsche Verlagsbuchhandlung, 1989), 12. It has no *Sanctus*. Some researchers speculate that since the manuscript was discovered several centuries after only in fragments, the *sanctus* could have been in the missing part of the manuscript. Cf. T. Klauser, *A Short History of the Western Liturgy*, 11.

goes on to recount the work of redemption and directly leads to the institution narrative and then anamnesis, epiclesis and doxology.[132] Cyprian of Carthage (248-249) in his writing *On the Sacrament of the Cup of the Lord* (Epistle 63) provides further insight to understand this prayer.[133] Cyprian uses the name "preface" for the introductory dialogue:

> Ideo et sacerdos ante orationem, præfatione præmissa, parat fratrum mentes dicendo: *Sursum corda,* ut dum respondet plebs: *Habemus ad Dominum,* admoneatur nihil aliud se quam Dominum cogitare debere.[134]

The eighth century manuscripts, the Gelasian sacramentary and the *Missale Francorum*, introduce the title *Incipit canon actionis* and then begin *"Sursum corda."* The *canon actionis* is "the norm of the action," the action in question being the Eucharist. The *canon actionis* includes the dialogue and preface.[135] In the Gregorian

---

[132] L. Deiss, *Springtime of the Liturgy*, 130. See also *On the Apostolic Tradition,* trans. A. S. Sykes (New York: St. Vladimir's Seminary Press, 2001). The Eucharist was continuous from dialogue to final Amen.

Hans Lietzmann, the Berlin liturgical historian's analysis of Hippolytus' Eucharistic prayer reveals that it is direct development from the churches of St. Paul and the present structure of preface is similar to this ancient text in several aspects. Cf. T. Klauser, *A Short History of the Western Liturgy,* 16. See also R. Moloney, *Our Eucharistic Prayers in Worship, Preaching and Study*, Theology and Life Series 14 (Wilmington, Delaware: Michael Glazier, 1985), 48.

[133] A. Dirksen, *Elementary Patrology: The writings of the Fathers of the Church* (St. Louis, Mo.: B. Herder Book Co., 1959), 71.

[134] *De dominica oratione* 31, in Cor.Pr, IX-X. "Before the prayer, the priest, in a preliminary preface [*præfatione præmissa*], prepares the minds of the brethren, saying, *Sursum corda,* so that when the people reply *Habemus ad Dominum* they realize they must think only of the Lord." This English translation is cited from J. Lionel, *Let us celebrate* (Bangalore, India: Asian Trading Corporation, 2006), 67.

[135] J. Jungmann, *The Mass of the Roman Rite,* vol. 2, 103.

Sacramentary, the term 'preface' is also applied to the *Hanc igitur* ("We therefore beg you to accept...") and to the blessings that precede the final doxology. From these examples, we can say that *Præfatio* means "prayer or solemn proclamation during public worship."[136]

4.2.2. The Character of the Text known as "Preface"

In the Latin tradition, the preface has a unique character due to its function.[137] Anthony Ward identifies three functions: "didactic," "evocative," and "proclamatory,"[138] whereas, Henry Ashworth identifies, "thanksgiving" and "praise" for redemption.[139] These two observations contribute toward a better understanding of its role. As the liturgical year unfolds,[140] the preface expresses the motive of thanksgiving[141] according to a particular aspect of the *mirabilia Dei*.[142] Preface does not merely express but evokes and brings salvation.[143] It "proclaims the faith of the Church"[144] calling to mind

---

[136]E. Mazza, *The Eucharistic Prayers of the Roman Rite*, 38.

[137] P. Bruylants, LMD 87 (1966): 115.

[138] S.Comp, 14.

[139] H. Ashworth, *I nuovi prefazi*, 759.

[140] This refraction of the whole mystery of salvation through the prism of the liturgical year yields a series of texts that relate each stage of that cycle to the core of it namely, the Paschal Mystery.

[141] L. Bouyer, LMD 87 (1966): 99. L. Bouyer recommends that in order to understand the function and character of the prefaces we must go to the roots in the Jewish *berakoth*, thanksgiving to God for the creation and all his marvelous deeds in the history. The preface plays the role of the Prologue of John's gospel. As the prologue in the gospel prepares to understand the mystery of Incarnation and God's plan of salvation fulfilled in Jesus Christ, the preface determines the attitude in which the assembly sacramentally participates in the sacrifice of Christ. It is a prayer of thanksgiving.

[142] S.Comp, 14.

[143] P. Bruylants, LMD 87 (1966): 115.

[144] S.Comp, 14.

the history of salvation actualized through the celebration of the mystery. This makes prefaces something unique with interwoven images of redemption expressed with lyricism[145] found nowhere else in the prayers of the Roman Missal.[146] It brings the vivid memories of the past in the history of salvation here and now and orients them to the future.[147]

4.2.3. The Structure of Preface

A preface is made up of five essential elements: "the introductory dialogue, the protocol, the embolism, the eschatocol, and the acclamation, *Sanctus*."[148] The introductory dialogue refers to the initial greeting, the protocol refers to the opening statement, the embolism refers to the main body of the preface, the eschatocol refers to the mention of angelic choirs and the acclamation refers to the hymn *Sanctus*.

1) The introductory dialogue consists of threefold invitation by priest celebrant and appropriate response by the congregation. The biblical and theological meaning will be discussed in the next chapter when we consider changes in the translation of the new edition of the Missal.

2) The opening statement is the beginning of preface. The opening sentence is a masterpiece of logical and doctrinal cohesion. The prayer begins with thanksgiving addressing directly the Father

---

[145] A. Griffiths, *We Give You Thanks and Praise* (Franklin, WI.: Sheed and Ward, 1999), xvi. See also Congregation for Divine Worship and Discipline of Sacraments, *Liturgiam Authenticam: Fifth instruction on Vernacular Translation of the Roman Liturgy* (Washington, DC.: USCCB, 2001), 97.

[146] It is different from other *Oratio* in the missal. Cf. H. Ashworth, *I nuovi prefazi*, 759-760.

[147] S.Comp, 14.

[148] Although different authors use different titles for these five constitutive elements of the prefaces I choose to use the titles used by A. Ward and C. Johnson from the Congregation for Divine Worship. Cf. S.Comp, 14.

and resting upon the mediation of Christ the sovereign high priest. The praise and thanksgiving in the liturgy is offered to the Father in and through Jesus Christ our Lord. This Christological dimension of liturgy is acknowledged verbally in the phrase, "through Christ our Lord" (*per Christum Dominum nostrum*). That is why in redaction criticism of liturgical texts the genuineness of the prayers in the Roman rite is recognized by Christ's high-priestly mediation,[149] expressed in this phrase.[150]

3) Generally, the main body of the preface is more elaborate than the other parts. The body of the text always articulates reasons for giving thanks and the particular liturgical season or feast dictates the theme.[151] The main body of the prefaces includes biblical allusions appropriate to the liturgical seasons and the mysteries celebrated.

4) Eschatocol serves as transition from the main body to the *Sanctus*. The idea of the angelic choirs in the presence of the Lord is repeated many times in the scriptures.[152] Hence, joining voices with the angels during liturgy is just and right, as we acknowledge the divine presence in the liturgy.

5) The hymn *Sanctus* comes at the end of the preface.

4.2.4. *Sanctus*

In the hymn *Sanctus*, one can see the obvious reference to the vision of the prophet Isaiah (Is 6:1-6). Some examples of research on the *Sanctus* can shed light on its historical and theological

---

[149] Pius XII, *Mediator Dei* #20 in C. Carlen, *The Papal Encyclicals 1939-1958*,122. See also SC #7 in Flannery, 120-121.

[150] P. Bruylants, LMD 87 (1966): 117-118. See also T. Klauser, *A Short History of the Western Liturgy*, 30-32.

[151] A. Croegaert, *The Mass: A Liturgical Commentary,* vol. 2 (Westminster, MD.: The Newman Press, 1959), 168.

[152] Gen 3:24, 28:10-22, Ex 25:17-22, Ps 103:20, 148:2, Is 6:1-5, Jn 1:51, Heb 12:22, Rev 4:2-11.

significance in preface.[153] Several studies affirm that from the earliest period, the *Sanctus* formed part of the Latin Eucharistic thanksgiving in the Roman, Gallican, Ambrosian and Mozarabic liturgies. However, the so-called *anaphora* of Hippolytus (3rd Century) in its reconstruction does not include the *Sanctus*.[154] Based on this observation, Gregory Dix[155] suggests that the *Sanctus* did not belong to the ordinary of the Mass during the third century. He argues that it interrupts the flow of thought between the preface and *Te igitur*.[156] Agreeing with Gregory Dix, Enrico Mazza also argues for the absence of the *Sanctus*.[157]

In contrast to the arguments by Dix and Mazza, Eisenhofer affirms the universality of the use of the *Sanctus*[158] based on the letter of St. Clement (†101) to the Corinthians, where there is obvious reference to the *trisagion*. Clement does not mention explicitly that he is referring to the Eucharistic prayer, but one may logically conclude from his words that he indeed uses the contemporary liturgical text to make his point clear to the Corinthians.

---

[153] For more details on *Sanctus,* see Spinks, B., *The Sanctus in the Eucharistic Prayer* (New York: Cambridge University Press, 1991) and Ratclif, E. C., *Liturgical Studies* (London: S.P.C.K., 1976).

[154] B. Botte, *La Tradition apostolique de Saint Hippolyte,* LQF 39, 12. See also P. F. Bradshaw, et.al., *The Apostolic Tradition* (Minneapolis, MN.: Fortress Press, 2002) Some researchers argue that since only the fragments of the original manuscript of the *Apostolic Tradition* (Egyptian Church Order) were discovered, the *Sanctus* could have been in the missing part of the manuscript. Cf. T. Klauser, *A Short History of the Western Liturgy,* 17.

[155] G. Dix, *The Shape of the Liturgy* (London: A & C Black, 1986), 537.

[156] G. Dix, The treatise on the Apostolic tradition of St. Hippolytus of Rome, bishop and martyr (London: Society for Promoting Christian Knowledge, 1968).

[157] E. Mazza, *The Eucharistic Prayers of the Roman Rite,* 47.

[158] Eisenhofer, *Handbuch der Liturgik* in A. Croegaert, *The Mass,* vol. 2, 179.

We should note how the whole throng of his angels stands ready to serve his will. For Scripture says: "Ten thousand times ten thousand stood by him, and thousands of thousands minister to him and cried out: Holy, holy, holy is the Lord of Hosts: all creation is full of his glory."[159] [Dan 7:10, Is 6:3]

Similarly, early Christian writers such as Tertullian and Origen allude to the *Sanctus* in their writings.[160] The following two examples offer further support for the theological significance of *Sanctus* in the Tradition. During the Arian heresy the Fathers of the Church used the evidence of "Holy Holy Holy…" in the liturgy as a witness for Trinitarian interpretation.[161] St. Gregory of Nyssa adjures catechumens: "Hasten, that you may be able to sing with the faithful what the Seraphim sing."[162] From these examples, one can surmise that if Hippolytus chose to omit the *Sanctus* from his scheme, it may be because he was particularly interested in conveying the celebrant's part, whereas the people's part was already familiar and no reference to it was needed.[163]

The *Sanctus* was found in the Eastern tradition as early as 350 AD. Cyril of Jerusalem (314-387) in his fifth *Mystagogical*

---

[159] Clement of Rome *Letter to the Corinthians* 34,6 in C. C. Richardson. ed., *Early Christian Fathers* (New York: Touchstone Book, 1996), 59. The contemporary biblical scholars are of the opinion that in all probability Prophet Isaiah would have been quoting the existing the liturgical hymn used in the temple of Jerusalem. Like many of the apocalyptic hymns of the liturgy of that time were transposed to heavenly scenario in the visions, this hymn also was used at the time of Isaiah. Cf. L. Bouyer, LMD 87 (1966): 107.

[160] *De Oratione,* 3. in H. Bettenson, *The Early Christian Fathers* (Oxford: Oxford University Press, 1978), 158. See also L. Bouyer, LMD 87 (1966): 107.

[161] A. G. Martimort, ed., *The Church at Prayer,* vol. 2, vol. 2, 95.

[162] *De Bapt.* in PG, 46.

[163] G. Nicholls, "The History of the Prayers of the Roman Canon," *Theological and Historical Aspects of the Roman Missal*, 38.

Catechesis on Eucharist clearly mentions this acclamation in the following words:

> After this we make mention of heaven, earth...angels, archangels, powers, dominations, principalities, virtues, thrones, and Cherubim with their many faces...we also make mention of the Seraphim, whom Isaiah contemplated when he was caught up in an ecstasy by the Holy Spirit. They encircled the throne of God...And they were exclaiming: Holy, holy, holy is the Lord Sabaoth! We sing this doxology, which comes to us from the Seraphim, in order that we may participate in the song of the heavenly armies.[164]

Various scholars have found evidence for the widespread use of the *Sanctus*. Based on the papyrus discovered at Der Balyzeh, Schermann claims that the ancient Egyptian liturgy contained a Eucharistic Prayer with *Sanctus* and that the Verona liturgy is a summary of it.[165] There is also evidence that the *Sanctus* was sung in the second half of the fourth century in the liturgy of the *Apostolic Constitutions* (composed at Antioch about 381), in the Egyptian anaphora of Serapion and Der Balyzeh.[166] The treatise by pseudo-Athanasius, *De Trinitate et de Spiritu Sancto*,[167] bears witness

---

[164] Cyril of Jerusalem, *Cat.*23,6. quoted in L. Deiss, *Springtime of the Liturgy,* 285.

[165] L. Deiss, *Springtime of the Liturgy,* 243, 246. See also A. Croegaert, *The Mass,* vol. 2, 178.

[166] M. Metzger, trans., *Les Constitutions Apostoliques,* VIII, 12:5,27 in S.Chr, vol. 336, 179-193.

[167] This treatise by pseudo-Athanasius was one of the sources of *De Trinitate* ascribed to Didymus the Blind. Cf. A. Heron, "Some Sources used in the *De Trinitate* ascribed to Didymus the Blind," R. Williams, ed., *The Making of Orthodoxy* (Cambridge, UK: Cambridge University Press, 1989), 173.

that "all Christ's churches from East to West confess that the Father is worthily praised by the seraphim."[168]

In the West, the first appearance of the *Sanctus* is traced to around the year 400 AD. Half a century later, we find that the custom of including the *Sanctus* has become general practice. The verse "Blessed is he who comes in the name of the Lord" (*Benedictus*), is preceded and followed by the acclamation *Hosanna in the highest*[169] and this verse was added later throughout the West.[170] Cæsarius of Arles (473-540) mentions the addition of the *Benedictus* for the first time. This addition in the West spread to the East during the eighth century.[171] While the *Sanctus* is addressed directly to God, the *Benedictus* focuses on Christ, since it evokes the Lord's triumphant entry into Jerusalem. The *Benedictus* is a Psalm verse (Ps 118:26), which was a popular processional hymn used during the feast of tabernacles, celebrating the presence of the Lord in the Old Testament.[172]

4.2.5. Number of Prefaces

Since preface is a variable text in the Mass that suits the mystery or feast celebrated, it enlarges upon the reason for thanksgiving for a particular aspect of the marvelous deed of God in the history of salvation; hence the variety of prefaces in Latin liturgical tradition. The more ancient we go, the more number of prefaces we see in the sacramentaries. However, during the reign of St. Gregory the Great (+604), the number of prefaces was reduced to

---

[168] Dr. Schermann, *Aegypt. Abendmahlsliturgien des I Jahrtausend* (Schoningh, Paderborn, 1912) in A. Croegaert, *The Mass,* vol. 2, 178.

[169] Ps 118:25-26; Mt 21:9.

[170] Benedictus in the *Sanctus* is a Christian addition to the messianic Psalm 118, which was already used, in the Jewish thanksgiving. Cf. L. Bouyer, LMD 87 (1966): 108.

[171] A. G. Martimort, ed., *The Church at Prayer*, vol. 2, vol. 2, 95-96.

[172] L. Soubigou, *A Commentary on the Prefaces,* 13-14.

nine. The number was gradually increased in the subsequent centuries. The following table[173] sheds light to understand the variation in number of prefaces used in various sacramentaries from the different centuries.

Sacramentary	Liturgical source	Number of Masses	Number of Proper Prefaces
Mozarabic	Mozarabic Sacramentary	157	157
Gallican Sacramentaries	Missale Gothicum (7th Cent)	68	68
	Missale Reichenau (7th Cent)	11	15
	Missale Gallicanum (7th Cent)	20	18
	Missale Francorum (7th Cent)	13	10
	The Bobbio Missal (8th Cent)	62	76
Roman Sacramentaries	Sacramentarium Leonianum (6th Cent)	281	269
	Sacramentarium Gelasianum (8th Cent)	270	58
	Sacramentarium Gregorianum (Muratori – 9th Cent)	259	87
	Liber Sacramentorum (Menard - 10th Cent)	291	214
Ambrosian	Ambrosian Missal	336	263

After the Council of Trent, the liturgical reform reduced the prefaces to fifteen due to several corruptions in the text, but in the following centuries new prefaces were added. Even when the number was restricted, some special provisions were made for some regions to use additional prefaces. For example, France always preserved several such additional prefaces. By 1961 France had 52 prefaces including diocesan proper.[174] Such provisions already appeared in the MR 1962 approved for France.[175] In the 1962 Missal

---

[173] A. Croegart, *The Mass*, vol. 2, 169.

[174] J. Poilly, "Les préfaces parisiennes: la préface de S. Jean Baptiste," EL 77 (1963): 101-108.

[175] P. Jounel, "Le nouveau propre de France," LMD 72 (1962): 141-165, "Les sources françaises du missel de Paul VI," QL 4 (1971): 305-316.

of John XXIII we see twenty prefaces. Following the model of the ancient sacramentaries, the liturgical reform after Vatican II increased the number of prefaces to eighty-four. Priest can take advantage of these enhanced choices of prefaces for various occasions in the Roman Missal and use them on appropriate occasions for the intense spiritual renewal in the parish.

4.6. Eucharistic Prayer - Highpoint of the Celebration

4.6.1. Historical Notes

If we keep in mind that the word "Eucharist" means "thanksgiving," the prayer of the *Didache* may be called the oldest "Eucharistic" prayer in the Christian Tradition. It surely originated in the atmosphere of Jewish worship, and specifically in the world of Jewish blessings for the community meals. This prayer served as mealtime prayer for the faithful who gathered for the agape meals (I Cor 11:17-22). *Didache* says: "With regard to the Eucharist, give thanks in this manner: First, for the cup: "We thank you, our Father, for the holy vine of David your servant...' Then for the bread broken: 'We thank you, our Father, for the life and knowledge...'"[176]

St. Justin wrote in *Apologia*: "As we said earlier, when we have finished praying, bread, wine and water are brought up. The president then prays and gives thanks according to his ability. And the people give their assent with an 'Amen.'"[177] Another important source is *Euchology,* the work of Serapion, Bishop of Thmuis who lived around 343 AD when the Council of Sardica was convened. According to St. Jerome, Serapion united both a great holiness of life and a brilliant intelligence which won him the surname *scholasticus,* "scholar." His work was discovered in 1894 at Mount Athos and ever since, it has received attention of theologians and liturgists. This work is a collection of thirty ritual prayers. Among

---

[176] *Didache* 9-10, in L. Deiss, *Spring time of the Liturgy,* 74-76.

[177] *Apologia* I, 67 in L. Deiss, *Spring time of the Liturgy,* 93.

them the ancient form of anaphora also appears, which attracts our interest.[178] The prayer begins with praise: "It is right and just to praise you, to celebrate you, to glorify you, eternal Father of the only begotten Son, Jesus Christ." These words are similar to the words and expressions we use today at the beginning of preface. The prayer goes further:

> Lord of the powers, fill this sacrifice too with your power and your participation. ...For the Lord Jesus, the night when he was betrayed, took bread, broke it, and gave it to his disciples saying: 'Take and eat, this is my body, which is broken for you for the forgiveness of sins.'...We offer too the cup, the figure of the blood. For the Lord Jesus, after the meal, took the cup and said to his disciples: 'Take and drink, this is my blood poured out for you, for the forgiveness of sins.'[179]

The prayer continues with a memento to the living and the dead and ends with final prayer and doxology. This prayer sheds light to understand the formulation of Eucharistic prayers that we use now. The sacrificial character of Eucharistic prayer is acknowledged in the words of this prayer.

At the last supper Christ instituted the sacrifice and paschal meal that make the sacrifice of the cross continuously present in the Church, when the priest, representing Christ the Lord, carries out what the Lord did and handed over to his disciples to do in his memory (GIRM 78). Christ took the bread and the cup and gave thanks; he broke the bread and gave it to his disciples, saying: "Take and eat, this is my body." Giving the cup, he said: "Take and drink, this is the cup of my blood. Do this in memory of me." Accordingly, the Church has planned the celebration of the Eucharistic liturgy around the parts corresponding to these words and actions of Christ:

---

[178] *The Euchology of Serapion of Thmuis,* 13 in L. Deiss, *Spring time of the Liturgy,* 193.

[179] Ibid.

- In the preparation of the gifts, the bread and the wine with water are brought to the altar, that is, the same elements that Christ used.

- In the Eucharistic prayer thanks is given to God for the whole work of salvation and the gifts of bread and wine become the body and blood of Christ.

Through the breaking of the one bread the unity of the faithful is expressed and through communion, they receive the Lord's body and blood in the same way the apostles received them from Christ's own hands.

4.6.2. Sacrificial Nature of Mass Expressed in Eucharistic Prayer

The council of Trent solemnly proclaimed the sacrificial nature of the Holy Mass which suits very well with the Tradition of the church. It was reaffirmed by Vatican II in its Constitution on Sacred Liturgy in the following words:

At the Last Supper our Savior instituted the Eucharistic sacrifice of his body and blood. He did this in order to perpetuate the sacrifice of the cross throughout the centuries until he should come again and in this way to entrust to his beloved Bride, the Church, a memorial of his death and resurrection (SC 47).

The Council's teaching is expressed constantly in the formularies of the Mass. This teaching, in the concise words of the Leonine Sacramentary, is that "the work of our redemption is carried out whenever we celebrate the memory of this sacrifice" (SC. 102). This teaching on the sacrificial nature of Mass is aptly and accurately brought out in the Eucharistic prayers. At the anamnesis or memorial, the priest, addressing God in the name of all the people, offers in thanksgiving the holy and living sacrifice: the Church's offering and the Victim whose death has reconciled us with God (PO.5, SC.10). The priest also prays that the body and blood of Christ may be a sacrifice acceptable to the Father, bringing salvation to the whole world (SC 14).

4.6.3. Prayers and Other Parts Assigned to the Priest

GIRM (n.30) says that among the parts assigned to the priest, the Eucharistic prayer is preeminent. Next are the prayers: the opening prayer or collect, the prayer over the gifts, and the prayer after communion. The priest, presiding over the assembly in the person of Christ, addresses these prayers to God in the name of the entire holy people and all present (SC 33). Thus there is good reason to call them "the presidential prayers." The priest who celebrates Mass takes it seriously, to pronounce the words in the Eucharistic prayer meaningfully with devotion and understanding. The Eucharistic prayer calls for all to listen in silent reverence, but also to take part through the acclamations for which the rite makes provision. The mention of the name of the Supreme Pontiff and the diocesan Bishop in the Eucharistic Prayer is not to be omitted, since this is a most ancient tradition that manifests ecclesial communion (GIRM 149). For "the coming together of the Eucharistic community is at the same time a joining in union with its own Bishop and with the Roman Pontiff."

4.6.4. Deacon's Role During Eucharistic Prayer

What is the role of the deacon during the Eucharistic prayer? The GIRM (n.134) states that, "During the Eucharistic prayer, the deacon stands near but slightly behind the priest, so that when necessary he may assist the priest with the chalice or the missal. At the final doxology of the Eucharistic prayer, the deacon stands next to the priest, holding up the chalice as the priest raises the paten with the Eucharistic bread, until the people have said the acclamation: *Amen*" (GIRM 179-180).

4.6.5. Options for Eucharistic Prayers

The new Roman missal gives several choices of Eucharistic prayers and some are formulated for specific occasions. Each choice of Eucharistic prayer has some uniqueness.

Eucharistic Prayer I (GIRM 219-225)

The first Eucharistic Prayer which is known as *the Roman Canon* is one of the most ancient and venerable among Church's patrimony of Eucharistic Prayers. Although some consider the date of this prayer as fourth century there are others who argue for much earlier date based on the elements in the prayer. It is impressive to think that generations of saints and simple Christians have prayed this prayer from the very early stages of the Western Christianity. The quality of solemnity of this Eucharistic Prayer is manifested in the sacred language in which the prayer is couched, especially with two special emphases on the themes of petition and sacrifice. Furthermore, the very fact that it is the longest of all the other Eucharistic Prayers in the Roman Missal attests to its solemn character.

The liturgical reform after Vatican II has slightly modified the text of this Eucharistic prayer. For example, the list of saints has been shortened. As far as rituals concerned, the twenty five signs of the cross used earlier and two kisses of the altar are eliminated.[180] This Eucharistic prayer consists of many wonderful forms explaining the theology of the Eucharist. That is why Cipriano Vagaggini's study has shown how the importance given to the Roman Canon helped to preserve Christian doctrines in the midst of attacks and challenges from Protestant reformers during the sixteenth century.[181] Since this prayer is slightly longer, some priests do not use it often. It is recommended that the priests understand the richness in this prayer and use it more often. This Eucharistic prayer is more appropriate for solemnities and occasions like, Christmas & during the octave, Epiphany, Holy Thursday, From Easter vigil to second Sunday of Easter inclusive, Ascension and Pentecost, because it

---

[180] Adolf Adam, *The Eucharistic Celebration, the Source and Summit of Faith* (Collegeville, Minnesota: The Liturgical Press, 1994).

[181] C. Vagaggini, "Le Canon Roman et la réforme liturgique," LMD 87 (1966): 134.

has special form for *Hanc igitur* (Father accept this offering) and
Quam oblationem (Bless and approve our offering) for Holy
Thursday and Easter vigil to the second Sunday of Easter inclusive.
Besides these examples, there are different forms given for other
solemnities. This is the uniqueness of this first Eucharistic prayer.
Several names of the saints are mentioned in this Eucharistic prayer.
When the feast/memorial of the saint mentioned in the Eucharistic
prayer are commemorated, it is advisable to use this Eucharistic
prayer.

Eucharistic Prayer II (GIRM 226-228)

The second Eucharistic Prayer is a reworking and revision of
the Eucharistic prayer which is attributed to Hippolytus (3rd century).
The *Sanctus,* missing in Hippolytus' manuscript is added in the
present text. The epiclesis of the Holy Spirit is also added. The
second Eucharistic prayer expresses well the epiclesis: "Let your
Sprit come upon these gifts to make them holy, so that they may
become for us the body + and blood of our Lord, Jesus Christ."[182]
The invocation of the Holy Spirit is sought not only on the gifts but
also on the community: "May all of us who share in the body and
blood of Christ be brought together in unity by the Holy Spirit."[183]
The order of some sections has also been changed. With reference
to its source, it has been called the "Eucharistic prayer from the
time of the martyrs." This form is shorter and more often used,
because of the masterful way in which it combines depth of thought
with simplicity and consciousness of expression. Eucharistic Prayer
II has features that make it particularly suitable for weekdays and
special circumstances. Although it has its own preface, it may also
be used with other prefaces, especially those that summarize the
mystery of salvation, such as the Sunday prefaces or the common
prefaces.

---

[182] Eucharistic Prayer II – Roman Missal.
[183] Ibid.

Eucharistic Prayer III (GIRM 229-231)

The origin of the third Eucharistic Prayer is more easily documented then the other three principal Eucharistic Prayers. Cipriano Vagaggini who was responsible for Coetus X, the study group of the Consilum that supervised the revision of Eucharistic Prayers informs us that his intention was to compose a canon which would be at once contemporary and traditional. He said, "an original composition which, with all due regard for the literary and liturgical style proper to an anaphora, would seek to come as close as possible to what biblical, traditional, liturgical and pastoral feeling suggests as the ideal for today in this field."[184] Although some call this as the Eucharistic Prayer of Vatican II, one should not think that it is formed by the men of that council, but rather the important concerns of the council provided key to the content of this prayer.

This Eucharistic prayer begins with unity of believers in worshiping God. This prayer is preferred for Mass during Sundays and feasts. This prayer does not have its own preface, hence it may be used with any other prefaces given in the Missal according to the occasion of the celebration. In the funeral masses either Eucharistic Prayer II or III is chosen because the text offers provision to mention the name of the person diseased. This prayer also conveys epiclesis in clearer terms: "And so Father, we bring you these gifts. We ask you to make them holy by the power of your Spirit, that they become the body + and blood of your son, our Lord Jesus Christ, at whose command we celebrate this Eucharist."

Eucharistic Prayer IV (GIRM 232-236)

The fourth Eucharistic Prayer is generally considered as the most biblical of all the other Eucharistic Prayers, because it recalls the entire salvation history. This Eucharistic prayer draws heavily on the traditions of the Eastern Church, especially the Apostolic

---

[184] C. Vagaggini, *The Conon of the Mass and Liturgical Reform* (London: Chapman, 1967), 123.

Constitutions of Antioch and Byzantine Liturgy of St. Basil. As a
general pattern, in the Roman tradition the recollection of the salvation
history is confined to the Prefaces focusing one aspect according to
the liturgical season. On the contrary, the Eastern Eucharistic Prayers
always have this synthetic presentation of salvation history. Thus
following the model of an ancient prayer traditionally associated
with St. Basil, this fourth Eucharistic Prayer in our Roman Missal
sums up the history of salvation from creation to the paschal mystery,
coming of the Holy Spirit and continuation of God's work on earth
through the believers. It charts out the mission program of Jesus,
proclaiming the good news to the poor and liberation to the captives.
This Eucharistic Prayer has its own preface and the flow of the text
demands that only this preface can be used with this prayer. Due to
the structure of this prayer no special formulary for the dead may
be inserted.

Eucharistic Prayer for Children

The new missal provides choice of three Eucharistic prayers
for the Masses with children. All these three Eucharistic prayers
have their own preface composed according to the level of
understanding of children. The first Eucharistic Prayer for Children's
Mass is simple and short. It has prayers to be said by the main
celebrant and concelebrants.

The second Eucharistic Prayer for Children's Mass is
composed in the pattern of prayer by the main celebrant and response
by the children. It gives opportunity for the children to involve actively
in the prayer and it is more participatory. It also helps the children to
be attentive during the Mass. The third Eucharistic Prayer for
Children's Mass has special prayers for various liturgical seasons
especially the season of Easter. This prayer also follows the pattern
of prayer by the celebrant and response by the children. These
prayers provide opportunity for the children to develop interest in
the Eucharistic liturgy at the very early stage of their life because of
the participatory design of the Eucharistic Prayer. This prayer is
aptly used in the context of school Mass and also Mass for children
in the parish.

Eucharistic Prayer for Masses of Reconciliation

In the new missal there are two choices of Eucharistic prayers for the masses of reconciliation. Like children's mass, this Eucharistic prayer also has a preface of its own.

The first Eucharistic prayer for Masses of Reconciliation recalls the covenant and draws attention to God's love and mercy and his readiness to forgive sinners. The focus is, the individual sinner's broken friendship with God because of sin and invitation to renew this friendship by seeking God's forgiveness, trusting in His mercy. The whole mood is that the sinner receives forgiveness and in gratitude he sings the hymn of praise.

The second Eucharistic prayer for Masses of Reconciliation addresses the conflict and division in the minds of the people and calls for peace in Jesus Christ. It has a social dimension seeking the community of believers to be reconciled among themselves and with God. The prayer invites to put away vengeance and forgive each other as we all have received God's forgiveness. It concludes with prayer to gather people of every race, language and way of life to share in the one eternal banquet. These prayers are used in parishes during the season of Lent or other appropriate occasions. Since there are so much broken relationships in the society and in the families, such prayers would be appealing and would call for true reconciliation among the members of the worshipping community.

5. Communion Rite

5.1. Communion Rite as the Culmination of the Celebration

In the earliest liturgies the celebrant had no fixed formula to say once the anaphora was over and the people had replied "amen." He only had gestures to make: to break the consecrated bread, consume the sacrifice in communion and distribute it to the people. These actions were not necessarily accompanied by prayers of the priest since he had already prayed for the communicants in the anaphora. Gradually, however, chants and fixed prayers were added to the actions.

In the new Order of the Mass the communion rite is seen as the organic culmination of the entire celebration and the highpoint of the participation of the faithful. Preparation for it takes the form of different rites which form a series of ordered units: the Lord's Prayer, embolism, rite of peace, the fraction or breaking of the bread and communion. Eucharistic celebration is the paschal banquet, hence it is desirable that in keeping with the Lord's command, his body and blood should be received as spiritual food by the faithful who are properly disposed. In this sense, the preparatory rites lead the faithful to the communion.

5.2. The Lord's Prayer

In the English Missal four versions of the introductory exhortation are given. After the main celebrant says the introductory exhortation, the entire congregation either sings or says the Our Father. The principle celebrant says the introductory exhortation with hands joined. He says or sings the Our Father with hands extended together with the concelebrants and people (GIRM 237). Either for reciting or singing the Our Father, only the text found in the Roman Missal is used. In the Lord's prayer a petition is made for daily food, which for Christians means preeminently the Eucharistic bread and also purification from sin, so that what is holy may, in fact be given to those who are holy (GIRM 81).

5.3. Embolism

The prayer "Deliver us O Lord..." is said by the principal celebrant alone with hands extended. All the concelebrants and the people say the acclamation, "For the kingdom..." (GIRM 238). The embolism enlarging upon the last petition of the Lord's Prayer itself, begs deliverance from the power of evil for the entire community of the faithful (GIRM 81). It asks for deliverance from evil and peace and ends with the eschatological note with the citation from St. Paul's letter to Titus 2:13: "as we wait in joyful hope for the coming of our Savior, Jesus Christ." The acclamation is an ancient practice in the Church which is attested in *Didache*. This is also found in some manuscripts of the Gospel of Mathew and traditionally follows the Lord's Prayer in most Eastern liturgies.

5.4. Rite of Peace

In this rite, the Church asks for peace and unity for herself and for the whole human family, and the faithful express to each other their ecclesial communion and mutual charity before communicating in the Sacrament (GIRM 82). After the people have replied to the celebrant's wish, the deacon or if there is no deacon, the priest himself exhorts them: "Let us offer each other the sign of peace." The principal celebrant exchanges the sign of peace with the concelebrants first and then to the deacon (GIRM 239). The members of the congregation exchange the sign of peace. The sign of peace is exchanged only to those who are nearest and in a sober manner (GIRM 82). This is precisely mentioned in the GIRM because it should not be an occasion for socializing, thus causing disturbance during the liturgy. The sign of peace is carried out with proper reverence, though it should not be unnecessarily prolonged, nor should it be accorded undue importance (GIRM 83).

5.5. Fraction or Breaking of the Bread

GIRM seeks to restore the original meaning of this action. Fraction is a sign that in sharing the one bread of life which is Christ, we who are many are made one body in Christ (I Cor. 10:17). Following Christ's gesture of breaking bread at the Last Supper which gave the entire Eucharistic Action its name in Apostolic times, the priest breaks the Eucharistic Bread, assisted by a deacon (if necessary) or one of the concelebrants. The breaking of the bread is done only after the Rite of peace and not before (GIRM 83, RS 73). The priest breaks the Bread and puts a piece of the host into the chalice to signify the unity of the Body and Blood of the Lord in the work of salvation, namely, of the living and glorious Body of Jesus Christ. The supplication *Agnus Dei* (Lamb of God) is either sung or recited which accompanies the fraction. For this reason GIRM even says that the invocation may be repeated as many times as necessary until the rite has reached its conclusion, but the last time, ending with the words *grant us peace* (GIRM 83). For the people, a more complete form of participation is to receive the body and blood of Christ. It is appropriate and highly encouraged that at least some pieces from the fraction are distributed in communion to the people. For convenience sake small hosts are used for communion to the people considering the large church attendance in our context. Such small hosts need not be broken (RS 49).

5.6. Immediate Preparation for Communion

It is appropriate that the actual communion be preceded by a moment of recollection. Meanwhile the priest chooses one of the two prayers which he says in a low voice. The faithful also pray in silence for a moment. The priest then shows the faithful the Eucharistic Bread, holding it above the paten or above the chalice and invites them to the banquet of Christ. Along with the faithful he then makes an act of humility using the prescribed words taken from the Gospel (GIRM 84). It is desirable that the people receive hosts consecrated in the same Mass as the priest does (GIRM 85, RS 89, *and Eucharisticum Mysterium* 31-32).[185] This gesture expresses the communion more vividly. However in some pastoral circumstances there may be some practical difficulties during which the priest can distribute communion kept in the tabernacle. While the priest is receiving the communion the choir can start the communion song. As the GIRM (86), says the purpose of this communion song is to express the communicants' union in spirit by means of the unity of their voices, to show joy of heart, and to highlight more clearly the 'communitarian' nature of the procession to receive communion. The song should be as far as possible known

---

[185] The Missal of 1570 encourages that the hosts destined for those approaching the holy table have been consecrated during the Mass in which they are participating. However, the actual medieval practice was to bring the hosts that were already consecrated. Cf. A. G. Martimort, ed., *The Church at Prayer*, vol. 2, vol. 2, 168.

to all the faithful. The communion procession should be in an orderly way.

5.7. Communion in the Body and Blood of Christ

The Constitution on the Liturgy determined that in certain circumstances the faithful might have access to the chalice; the change implied no derogation from the dogmatic principle laid down by the Council of Trent. The number of cases in which the new rite might be practiced was extended in 1970.[186] It is true that the reality received is the same whether a person received under one or both species. On the other hand, the sacrament's full wealth of meaning is brought out by the combined signs of bread and wine. In keeping with biblical symbolism, reception of the bread suggests above all a vital assimilation, nourishment for a journey, and fellowship at the same table. Reception of the cup conjures up a feast that gives a foretaste of the banquet in the kingdom. *Eucharisticum Mysterium* (n. 32), the Instruction issued by the Sacred Congregation for Rites says, "Holy communion has more complete form as a sign when it is received under both kinds." Same teaching is asserted by GIRM (281)[187] where we read, "Holy communion has a fuller form as a sign when it is distributed under both kinds." GIRM enumerates certain circumstances in which communion could be given under both species. Nevertheless, the GIRM and *Redemptonis Sacramentum* give some caution and guidelines for distributing communion under both species. GIRM specifies circumstances where communion under both species is permitted (GIRM 283-285). Nonetheless, such permission is given only after ensuring that there is no danger of profanation of the sacrament or the rite and provided the faithful are well instructed and trained. Many of Episcopal conferences have expressed a desire for authority to permit those of the faithful who wish to receive Communion in hand. This faculty

---

[186] See. Instruction *Sacramentali Communione*, June 1970.

[187] See also. Canon 925 and commentary. J. A. Coriden, T. Green and D. Heintschel, ed., *The Code of Canon Law – A Text and Commentary*, 658.

was given to the Episcopal conference if they asked for it.[188] The original custom of giving communion in hand was abandoned in the middle ages in order to show respect to the Eucharist. Those who requested permission to receive communion in hand thought this was a much more human gesture to extend the hand, as this action expresses a self commitment. The ritual proposed for Communion in the hand is inspired by the description given in ancient texts, especially in the Jerusalem catecheses from around the year 400 which says:

> When you come forward, do not draw near with your hands wide open or with the fingers spread apart; instead, with your left hand make a throne for the right hand, which will receive the king. Receive the body of Christ in the hollow of your hand and give the response: 'Amen.' ... Then, after sharing in the body of Christ, draw near also to the cup of his blood. Do not stretch out your hands, but bow in adoration and respect, and say: 'Amen.' Then sanctify yourself further by sharing in the blood of Christ.[189]

The Instruction by the Congregation for Divine Worship, *Redemptonis Sacramentum* (92) says,

Although each of the faithful always has the right to receive Holy Communion on the tongue, at his choice, if any communicant should wish to receive the Sacrament in the hand, in areas where the Bishops' Conference with the *recognitio* of the Apostolic See has given permission, the sacred host is to be administered to him or her. However, special care should be taken to ensure that the host

---

[188] See: Congregation for Divine Worship, in a notification of April 3, 1985.

[189] *Cat.* 23,22 (*The Catecheses of Cyril of Jerusalem*) in L. Deiss, *Spring time of the Liturgy*, 289. St. Cyril preached twenty four catecheses or instructions at the Basilica of Holy Sepulcher, Jerusalem around the year 350. These instructions are used much to study the Christian tradition and liturgy.

is consumed by the communicant in the presence of the minister, so that no one goes away carrying the Eucharistic species in his hand. If there is a risk of profanation, then Holy Communion should not be given in the hand to the faithful.

That is why it is recommended in large shrines where the priest /deacon /minister do not know all the faithful coming forward to receive Communion it is better to give Communion in tongue instead of hand. This is only to avoid any occasion for misuse. In other parishes, Communion could be distributed either in tongue or hand according to the wish of the communicant. The communicant also should come forward to receive it with respect and the appropriate gesture is extended hands in receiving form. The rite of communion traditionally requires the mediation of a minister, thus making it clear that a gift is being received. Under normal circumstances only Bishops and priests take the sacrament for themselves directly from the altar, the table of sacrifice. They are called "ordinary ministers" of Communion. Although deacon receives Communion from the Bishop or priest he can distribute Communion. There may be situations where there is not sufficient number of "ordinary ministers" for the task. In such circumstances the Church allows extraordinary ministers of the Communion. The Diocesan Bishop oversees such necessity and issues norms by which he determines the manner in which this function is to be carried out in accordance with the law, bearing in mind the tradition of the Church (RS 160). The extraordinary ministers could be chosen among men and women of reputed faith life and exemplary in character. Such extraordinary ministers have to be trained and instructed properly for this noble ministry that they are called to do. Any one cannot just walk into the sanctuary and take the ciboria to distribute Holy Communion. The extraordinary ministers should receive Holy Communion from the priest before they start to distribute to the people. Extraordinary ministers should not communicate to themselves. Although it is permissible for the extraordinary ministers to distribute Communion, when there are sufficient number of priests (ordinary ministers) to distribute Communion, the extraordinary ministers (although appointed by the bishop) need not come forward to distribute Communion (RS 88 & 157).

5.8. Prayer after Communion

To bring to completion the prayer of the people of God, and also to conclude the entire Communion Rite, the priest sings or says the Prayer after Communion in which he prays for the fruits of the mystery just celebrated. In the Mass only one prayer after Communion is said which ends with a shorter conclusion, that is: If the prayer is directed to the Father: *Through Christ our Lord* If it is directed to the Father, but the Son is mentioned at the end: *who lives and reigns forever and ever*; If it is directed to the Son: *You live and reign forever and ever.*

The people make the prayer their own by the acclamation: Amen (GIRM 89).

6. The Concluding Rite

The concluding rite consists of four elements:

- Greeting by the priest: *The Lord be with you* and the people's response: *And with your spirit.*

- Blessing: On some days and occasions, the Roman Missal provides enhanced formulary by way of Prayer Over the People. There are few solemn formulas given in the missal which could be used on such special occasions or solemnities. People certainly appreciate such blessings on special days like wedding mass, first Holy Communion, Sundays of Easter season, and parish feast.

- Dismissal of the people by the deacon or the priest so that each may go out to do good works, praising and blessing God.

- The kissing of the altar by the priest and the deacon, followed by a profound bow to the altar by the priest, deacon and other ministers (GIRM 90).

CHAPTER IV
NOTICEABLE CHANGES IN THE NEW MISSAL

The publication of the MR 2002 has several pastoral implications. First of all when the first English translation of MR 2002 is introduced in the parishes, both the pastors and congregation will hear new words and new expressions which are easily noticeable. Therefore if these words are not properly understood or explained well through systematic liturgical catechesis, they may lead to misunderstanding or some resentment. As we have seen in the previous chapters these prayers from the Roman Missal have come to us through a long tradition of Christian faith from the apostolic time to our own present age enriched with theological and liturgical condensation during every century in between the early Church and present time. Throughout the Tradition of the Church the words used in the Mass allude to a passage from Scripture, since liturgy has been understood in the Tradition as the actualization of the Word of God. Hence it presupposes contemplative attitude to grasp the meaning of these theologically crisp and rich words. Consequently the purpose of the liturgical catechesis on MR 2002 is not to win hostile debates or arguments over one or two words. When the communities hear new expressions during Mass according to the translation of MR 2002 they will be able to appreciate better the value of the faith that they profess. Though the MR 2002 is enriched with several profound textual and rubrical modifications, this chapter will try to identify only some examples of the easily noticeable changes in the prayers said in a parish context.

1. The New Title "Roman Missal" and not "Sacramentary"

As soon as the translation of MR 2002 comes into use any believer would notice change in the title. The English speaking Catholics have got used to see the Mass book with the title "Sacramentary." Particularly those who help in arranging for Mass, sacristans, servers and others must soon become familiar with the new title "Roman Missal." What is so important about this title? First of all the English translation "Roman Missal" is faithful translation of the Latin original *Missale Romanum*. Besides being sincere to the Latin title, the new title also has other valid reasons. In the first chapter of this book we have explained the evolution of the liturgical books from *Libelii* to Sacramentary and then to Missal. This historical explanation justifies the title "Roman Missal." In the liturgical tradition Sacramentary is collection of various prayers used during the Mass, whereas its later evolution Missal is one book that contains all the prayers and antiphons in a well organized fashion. The practical use of Sacramentary in the parishes became extinct almost from the eleventh century and was quickly replaced by the Missal. Hence the title "Roman Missal" is more appropriate to what is contained in the present MR 2002. It is known as "Roman Missal" because it is meant for the use of liturgy celebrated according to the Roman Rite (or Latin Rite) which is different from other liturgical rites such as Byzantine, Coptic, Greek Melkite, Armenian, Syro-Malabar , Syro-Malankara, etc.

2. Change in Style of the Language

In our human experience we engage with different organizations and institutions for our day to day life. For example the language style of a legal document is different from a story in a children's book. The style of writing in a text message over a mobile device is different from writing a doctoral dissertation. Every organization has some key expressions which are necessary to nurture the identity and mission of that organization and we perfectly understand that those key words can not be replaced with words used in simple street conversation. There are protocols in addressing civil dignitaries, and we are obliged to maintain certain decorum in the presence of the heads of the State such as President or Prime Minister of a country. Similarly liturgy has its own identity and its own style since "Liturgy is the Public worship which our Redeemer as Head of the Church renders to the Father, as well as the worship which the community of the faithful renders to its founder, and through him to the heavenly father. It is in short, the worship rendered by the Mystical Body of Christ in the entirety of its head and members."[190] That is why the sacred language in liturgy is a mystical language expressed in a language spoken by men. This mystical language cannot be merely reduced to some words in print or some gestures according to rubrics, but as we explained earlier the ritual language is symbolic language leading the worshiping community beyond what is in print and performed to a sacred reality.

In regard to style, the Catholics will notice three main changes when translation of MR 2002 comes out: 1) a more formal style of language than the language of ordinary conversation; 2) broader vocabularies; and 3) use of long sentences. These changes in the style presupposes careful reading on the part of priests who will be using these prayers during the celebration and diligent listening on the part of the assembly who are united with these prayers spiritually and respond to them. These changes imply some freshness in the sound and adjustments both on the part of the priest and assembly. This change in style of the translation is the result of observing the principles set forth by the Church document *Liturgiam Authenicam*[191] concerning translations of liturgical texts from Latin. Besides following this principle for authentic translation from the original, the long sentences have some benefits, because they help to connect the nuances in the profound words of the Missal which is weakened when the sentences are broken too much in order to shorten them. At this juncture one must acknowledge that the vernacular translation of the previous Missal had certainly helped all these years in the transition from Latin prayer to English prayer. It surely helped to understand the faith we professed. On the

---

[190] Pius XII, *Mediator Dei* Encyclical letter #20.

[191] Congregation for Divine Worship and Discipline of Sacraments, *Liturgiam Authenticam: Fifth instruction on Vernacular Translation of the Roman Liturgy* (Washington, DC.: USCCB, 2001).

foundation laid by this understanding, the translation of the MR 2002 attempts to enrich the liturgical text through reexamination of the Latin originals. The liturgical texts have their own literary genre; especially in Latin, the prayers have certain rhythm, poetry and sentiment. Considering this unique literary genre, a good translation implies more than right choice of words but a good translation requires expression of the same feeling in the original text. That is why those who have read classical or famous writings or novels in original languages get disappointed when the translation loses the force and feel of the story, especially when the translation deviates far from the original. Applying these principles from our human experience, we can notice that in some instances the prayers may sound more humble. Such a tone of prayer is appropriate considering the awesome presence of God. We are humans and we are not equal to God, yet as St. Paul acknowledges (Phil 2) He humbled Himself by becoming human, dying for our sins and rising to life so that we may be reunited with him. Some of the expressions in the translation will deliver this tone of Christian prayer very well. During the transition period there may be difficulties for some, nonetheless all Catholics will eventually begin to appreciate the text well, and soon the new text will become as familiar as the old one. We must also be reassured that the translation has come to us through a long process of very careful study, deliberations, reflections, discussions and supervision at national and international levels.

3. Prominent Changes in the Individual Parts of the Mass

In the translation of MR 2002 the Order of the Mass is not changed; it flows in the same way as we know after Vatican II. However there are some changes in the prayers said in the individual parts of the Mass such as, the Introductory Rites, Liturgy of the Word, Liturgy of the Eucharist and Concluding Rites.

3.1. Introductory Rites

In the previous chapter we explained the theological and liturgical significance of the Introductory Rites at the Mass which refers to all the prayers that we say and gestures we do from the first time we stand up at the beginning of the liturgy until we sit for the first time for the proclamation from Scripture. In the Introductory Rites of the new text we will see changes in the following: 1) Entrance Antiphon, 2) Penitential Rite / Rite of Blessing and Sprinkling of water, 3) Gloria and 4) concluding words of the Opening Prayer.

3.1.1. Entrance Antiphon

The Entrance Antiphon corresponds to a verse in the Bible for which reference is given in the Missal. These antiphons are selected according to the liturgical seasons, feasts of saints or intention of the liturgy for that particular celebration, like Mass for the various needs. If a parish has the practice of singing the entrance hymn in the place of Entrance Antiphons, one may not even notice the change in MR 2002. Since the words of the antiphons are changed, attention should be given when there is a custom of singing the antiphons in a parish.

3.1.2. Greeting and Response

After the priest makes the sign of the Cross, he greets the people with one of the three options given in the Missal. There was no change in the Latin original but the new translation makes it more faithful to the words found in the Scripture and the Latin original. There is no change in the first formula "The Lord be with you." However there are some slight alterations in the other two formulas based on the Pauline letters. One is the final words of St. Paul to the Corinthians (II Cor 13:13): "The grace of our Lord Jesus Christ, and the love of God and the communion of the Holy Spirit be with you all." The second is the frequent Pauline greetings found in his letters (Rom 1:7, I Cor 1:3): "Grace to you and peace from God our Father and the Lord Jesus Christ."

Until now the congregation used to respond to the greeting by saying: "And also with you." Soon the response would be "And with your spirit." Perhaps among all the changes in the Missal, several questions are raised regarding the significance and necessity for this change. Occasionally we read writings in non-academic journals criticizing this modification. However a careful evaluation explains the reason for the modified response in English. First of all the response "And with your spirit" is a faithful translation of its original in Latin which reads, "Et cum spiritu tuo." Several languages including French, Spanish, Italian and German have similar translation close to the Latin (e.g.: Spanish Missal. *"El Señor esté con vosotros: Y con tu espiritu."* Italian Missal: *Il Signore sia con voi: E con il tuo spirito.* French Missal: *Le Seigneur soit avec vous: Et avec votre esprit.*). Besides these general reasons there are deeper biblical and theological reasons as well for the change.

The traditional greeting in the liturgy, "The Lord be with you" (*Dominus Vobiscum*), is not a mere salutation such as "Hello" or "Good morning."[192] This salutation is a biblical greeting (Judg 6:12 [Angel greets Gideon], Ruth 2:4 [Boaz to the reapers], II Chr 15:2, Ps 129:7-8, Lk 1:28, II Thess 3:16). In a liturgical context, it is an invitation into the presence of God and it is a prayer for divine help to enter the task before us.[193] This greeting reminds us that we are entering a sacramental realm and alerts us of our responsibilities during the liturgy. In Exodus, we read one such vivid narration of the Lord making himself present in the hearing of his word and offering sacrifice.

> It shall be a regular burnt offering throughout your generations at the entrance of the tent of meeting before the Lord, where I will meet you to speak to you there. I will meet with the Israelites there, and it shall be sanctified by my glory...I will dwell among the Israelites, and I will be their God. And they shall know that I am the Lord their God... (Ex 29: 42-46).[194]

---

[192] This greeting was used when the divine message was delivered to the chosen people. It refers to God's blessings.

[193] See. Paul VI, *Mysterium Fidei* (Vatican, 1965) #35. See also GIRM #3,50,54,93 in LDS II, 7,29,30,47.

[194] See also the passage of Luke 24: 13-35 about the two disciples on the way to Emmaus.

The response to the greeting, "And with your spirit" (*Et cum spiritu tuo*) is a biblical formulation (II Tim 4:22, Gal 6:18, Phil 4:23, Philem 25). When St. Paul used this phrase, it was addressed to the Christian community. The Apostolic Tradition uses the same expression in its prayer.[195] In the liturgy, "spirit" refers to the work of the Holy Spirit in the priest/bishop in virtue of his ordination and traditionally this response is spoken only to ordained ministers.[196] That is why the *Missale Romanum* has preserved this biblical expression in all its texts. However, in 1970 The International Commission on English in the Liturgy (ICEL) translated this response as "And also with you." Though this previous translation conveys the meaning there is possibility of misunderstanding this phrase as simple greetings "how are you?" whereas the new translation is richer and clearer conveying the significance of the phrase.

3.1.3. Penitential Rite

The next change is in the words of the Penitential Rite. There are three options in the Missal for which the congregation responds by repeating the last phrase of the acclamation said by priest or deacon: Lord have mercy, Christ have mercy and Lord have mercy. Though there is no change in the response, there are some minor alterations in the formularies for the acclamations. The priests and deacons are to pay attention to the new words, but people continue to respond the same way as they are used to. During the Penitential Rite there are some changes when we say together the "Confiteor" which begins with the phrase: "I confess to almighty God." This prayer flows the same way except in a few places new expressions are added in the English following the original text. Hence if one is not careful at the introduction of the translation of MR 2002, it could cause some confusion. The following chart highlights the changes in bold letters:

---

[195] B. Botte, *La Tradition apostolique de Saint Hippolyte*, LQF, 12.

[196] R. Moloney, *Our Eucharistic Prayers in Worship, Preaching and Study*, 49. In the Eucharist, priest acts *in persona Christi*.

Present Text	Translation from MR 2002
I confess to almighty God, and to you, my brothers and sisters, that I have **sinned through my own fault** in my thoughts and words, in what I have done, and in what I have failed to do; **and** I ask blessed Mary ever virgin, and all the angels and saints, and you, my brothers and sisters to pray for me to the Lord, our God.	I confess to almighty God, and to you, my brothers and sisters, that I have **greatly sinned** in my thoughts and words, in what I have done, and in what I have failed to do, through **my fault, through my fault, through my most grievous fault; therefore** I ask blessed Mary ever virgin, and all the angels and saints, and you, my brothers and sisters to pray for me to the Lord, our God.

The new additions in the present translation express more elegantly the seriousness of our sins and sincerity of our contrition which is the purpose of the Penitential Rite. The new expressions in English clearly convey our humility in God's presence before proceeding deeper into the Eucharistic liturgy. The change does not make the present generation more sinful than the previous one. One must remember that the Latin original was the same and never changed. This seriousness of sin is maintained in most of the translations in other languages. The difference between translations in English and other languages does not mean that the non-English speaking believers were more sinful than English speaking believers. Now any misunderstanding about the sense of sin is rectified and it is made clear in the new translation adhering to the original text.

There is a complete retranslation of another rarely used option for the Penitential Act as given in the chart below:

Present Text	Translation from MR 2002
Priest: Lord, **we have sinned against you: Lord**, have mercy. All: **Lord, have mercy.** Priest: **Lord,** show us your mercy **and love.** All: And grant us your salvation.	Priest: **Have mercy on us, O Lord.** All: **For we have sinned against you.**Priest: Show us, O Lord, your mercy. All: And grant us your salvation.

At the end of the Penitential Act with "Confiteor" the priest proclaims absolution: "May almighty God have mercy on us / and lead us, with our sins forgiven / to eternal life." The translation of absolution will sound different now adhering to the original text in Latin. The slight change in the expressions avoids confusion with the absolution given at the Sacrament of Reconciliation.

There are some minor changes in the Rite of Blessing and Sprinkling of Holy Water, an option which is used on Sundays especially during the Easter season. Though these changes are not seen in the peoples' response, modifications are seen in the prayers said by the priest celebrant. The options for singing antiphons during the sprinkling are also now increased in number.

3.1.4. Gloria

The rubrical guidelines with regard to the use of Gloria remains the same; that is the hymn Gloria is either sung or recited on Solemnities and all Sundays of the year except during Advent and Lent. However the text of Gloria is changing now, and is slightly longer than the previous text. Hence it presupposes new music and practice by all who are involved. Two principles were followed in the revision of the new text: faithful to the words found in the Scripture and adhering to the sentiments expressed in the Latin original of MR 2002. For example the words, "his people on earth" is now changed to "people of good will" matching the biblical text (Lk 2:14). The new text, "We praise you, we bless you, we glorify you, we give you thanks for your great glory" expresses well the nature of the worship that we offer in the glorious presence of God. One word building on another may seem excessive, but it beautifully expresses the overwhelming experience that we could have in God's presence similar to the experience of the shepherds of Bethlehem when the angels sang Gloria and when they saw the Word incarnate lying in a manger (Lk 2:16-18). The previous expression "only Son of the Father" is changed to "Only Begotten Son...Son of the Father." Though the previous phrase expressed the same dogma that Jesus is the only Son of God, the grandeur of the doctrine is

somewhat unclear in the simple expression which is rectified in the
new text. The phrase "Only Begotten Son" is a faithful translation
of Latin *Fili Unigenite*. The word "sin" in the earlier translation is
changed as "sins" in the new text. The change makes it clear that
Jesus takes away not just generic sin from the world, but individual
sin. Jesus forgives personal sins of people.

3.1.5. Opening Prayer

After the Penitential Rite / Rite of Blessing and Sprinkling of
Holy Water and Gloria, the priest celebrant says the Opening Prayer
with the traditional invitation "Let us pray." The content of the
Opening Prayers for various liturgical seasons, feasts and occasions
are modified in the Latin original and completely retranslated. In the
next chapter we will study some examples of these significant
changes and their theological implications for a deeper understanding
of the MR 2002. The priest celebrants have to take note of these
changes. At the conclusion of the Opening Prayer there are also
changes in the usual formulary which now expresses the Trinitarian
communion more clearly and needs to be read diligently by the priest
celebrant.

3.2. The Liturgy of the Word

3.2.1. Readings and Response

The Liturgy of the Word includes all the scripture readings,
Homily, Profession of Faith (Creed) and General Intercessions. The
scripture readings during the Mass are proclaimed from Lectionary;
hence it does not come under the scope of our explanation of changes
in the Roman Missal. The readings are the same and the peoples'
response at the end of the proclamations would also be the same
except the response "And with your spirit" when the priest / deacon
says "The Lord be with you" before the gospel proclamation. The
reasons were explained earlier in the section on the Introductory
Rites. However the changes in the Roman Missal and their theological
and pastoral significance deserve attention in the Homily.

3.2.2. Homily

Homily explains the Word of God and helps to see its actualization in the present context. The homily can be based on Scripture or a part of the Holy Mass or a Mystagogy, explaining the sacred mysteries (SC 52, GIRM 13, 65). Since the changes in the words of the Missal have several pastoral implications, for first few months priests can incorporate the explanation of the Holy Mass into their Homilies, explaining to the congregation how the words of the Missal are rooted in Scripture and express our faith with more clarity.

3.2.3. Profession of Faith

There are considerable changes in the Profession of Faith; it does not mean that our faith is changing but it means that now the same faith that we professed until now is expressed in unambiguous terms, and rich in content. In the scripture readings and Homily people heard the marvelous deeds of God in the history of salvation and the actualization. Having heard the proclamation, now it is time for the entire worshiping community to respond to it by a Profession of Faith before the Eucharistic liturgy and by their faithful lives after (James 1:27). That is why it is important that all our voices are united to express one faith (Eph 4:5) in precise terms. During the Holy Mass usually the Nicene Creed is used. The history of Christian faith informs us how this Creed has developed in the midst of heresies and profound reflections and discussions at the Council of Nicaea (325 AD). The subsequent reflections by the Fathers of the Church and the Decrees of various Councils have profoundly explained the crystallization of the Christian dogma enshrined in this creed. Hence these words have come to us through the faithful Christian Tradition of all these centuries expressing the same faith. During the Holy Mass on Sundays and solemnities the rubric in the Roman Missal gives option either to use Niceno-Constantinopolitan creed (long form) or the baptismal symbol of the Roman Church, known as the Apostles' Creed. Since there are no changes in the Apostles' Creed, here we will examine the changes only in the Niceno-

Constantinopolitan creed. Here below we will see the changes in the Profession of Faith which help us to understand the theological significance of what we will be saying more clearly in the new translation.

Present Text	Translation from MR 2002
We believe in one God, the Father, the almighty, maker of heaven and earth, **of all that is seen and unseen.** **We believe** in one Lord, Jesus Christ, the **only** Son of God, **eternally begotten of the Father**, God from God, Light from Light, true God from true God, begotten, not made, **one in Being with the Father.** Through him all things were made. For us men and for our salvation he came down from heaven: **by the power of the Holy Spirit he was born of the Virgin Mary**, and became man. For our sake he was crucified under Pontius Pilate; **he suffered, died, and was buried. On the third day he rose again in fulfillment of the Scriptures;** he ascended into heaven and is seated at the right hand of the Father. He will come again in glory to judge the living and the dead, and his kingdom will have no end. **We believe** in the Holy Spirit, the Lord, the giver of life, who proceeds from the Father, and	**I believe** in one God, the Father, the almighty, maker of heaven and earth, **of all things, visible and invisible.** **And** in one Lord, Jesus Christ, the **Only Begotten** Son of God, **born of the Father before all ages**, God from God, Light from Light, true God from true God, begotten, not made, **consubstantial with the Father;** through him all things were made. For us men and for our salvation he came down from heaven **and by the Holy Spirit was incarnate of the Virgin Mary**, and became man. For our sake he was crucified under Pontius Pilate, **he suffered death and was buried, and rose again on the third day in accordance with the Scriptures.** He ascended into heaven and is seated at the right hand of the Father. He will come again in glory to judge the living and the dead, and his kingdom will have no end. **And** in the Holy Spirit, the Lord, the giver of life, who proceeds from the Father and the Son, **who** with the Father and the Son is **adored** and glorified, **who** has spoken through the Prophets. **And** one, holy, catholic and apostolic Church.

Present Text	Translation from MR 2002
the Son. With the Father and the Son he is **worshipped** and glorified. **He has spoken through the Prophets.** **We believe in** one holy catholic and apostolic Church. **We acknowledge** one baptism for the forgiveness of sins. **We look for** the resurrection of the dead, and the life of the world to come. Amen.	**I confess** one baptism for the forgiveness of sins **and I look forward to** the resurrection of the dead, and the life of the world to come. Amen.

In the new text soon we will notice change at the very beginning of the Creed; from "We believe" to "I believe." The new text is a literal translation of the Latin verb *Credo* (I believe) and consistent with post-Vatican II translations in many other languages throughout the world. For example the French text reads: *Je crois en un seul Dieu*..Though the Creed is the faith of the entire Church, the use of "I believe" asserts our personal faith together with other Christian believers from all over the world. The Latin verb *Credo* supplies the main verb for all the sentences that follow even when they are punctuated with periods. Similarly, in English the syntax "I believe" which is said together both by priest and congregation unifies all other parts of the Creed after the first sentence.

The translation also makes the faith clear in the new expression: "of all things visible and invisible." The previous words "seen and unseen" are replaced by "visible and invisible." In our human experience there are many things which are visible but not seen with our eyes. For example we are aware of the general hygienic advice to wash our hands to avoid spreading germs. These germs are still visible to our eyes when viewed under a microscope whereas they are unseen for our naked eyes. In contrast the invisible realities such as angels can not be seen even with special devices. Therefore when we profess that God is the maker "of all things visible and invisible" we include physical as well as super natural realities such as angels.

The expression "Only Begotten" in the new text appears also in the hymn Gloria. These words "Only Begotten" conveys very well the relation between the Father and the Son in the Holy Trinity. The previous expression "the only Son" does not have the same precision as the new translation. As this phrase continues, the new text changes from "eternally begotten of the Father" to "Born of the Father before all ages." Our faith in the Holy Trinity is that the Father and the Son existed from all eternity as revealed in the prologue of John's gospel (Jn 1:1-18). The Arian heresy taught that there was a time when the Son did not exist. This erroneous teaching was corrected by the Nicene Creed based on Scripture and the Tradition of Christian Faith. This phrase has a long history of development and crystallization of Christian dogma. That is why one has to be very careful to give precise expression in order to avoid repetition of the Arian misunderstanding in our own times.

One would find a new word "Consubstantial" in the forthcoming translation of MR 2002. This word is introduced to replace "one in being" in the previous translation. This word finds its place in the Creed to explain the relationship between Jesus and the Father. It is important to understand how Jesus relates to the Father, since heresies on this matter divided the Church in the early centuries. The word "Consubstantial" is matching the Latin word *consubstantialis* which means "having the same substance." As one can notice, "having the same substance," conveys deeper meaning than simply "one in Being." The word *consubstantialis* conveys well the divinity of Christ. This unique word is used only in the Creed. This word is preferred because the Councils in the history of the Church have coined precise words to articulate well the authentic Christian faith.

Another change in the Creed is the use of the word "Incarnate" instead of "born" in the present translation. Christians understand very well this unique word "incarnate" which has deeper meaning than the ordinary term "born." The use of the word "incarnate" precisely expresses our faith in the mystery of Incarnation. According the gospel account in Luke, Jesus was conceived by the power of the Holy Spirit (Lk 1:31,35). The new translation also makes it clear that Jesus became man not just at the birth but already at the very conception by the power of the Holy Spirit.

The previous expression "in fulfillment of the Scriptures" is changed to "In accordance with the Scriptures." Both these expressions convey the same meaning but the new translation is closer to the Latin original. This expression acknowledges that the resurrection of Jesus fulfills the OT prophesies and includes the NT witnesses for the Resurrection. There are a few other changes in terms matching the Latin text. For example, the new translation consistently replaces the word worship with adoration throughout the Missal adhering to the Latin term. In the Creed also the word "worshiped" is substituted by "adored." The phrase "We acknowledge" is replaced by "I confess" which is more forceful than the earlier one. One has to distinguish this word confess in the Creed which means "profess one's belief in" from usual understanding of confessing one's sins. In the history of the Church the term "Confessors" referred to those who witnessed for their faith through martyrdom. Another expression in the translation "I look forward to the resurrection" has a better tone of confidence and matches the Latin original.

3.3. The Liturgy of the Eucharist

3.3.1. Preparation of the Gifts

In the Preparation of the Gifts there are some minor textual corrections and insertion of punctuation at appropriate places. There are some changes in the order of words when the priest says the prayers. For example, the change occurs in the Blessing formula that the priest says holding the bread: "Blessed are you, Lord God of all creation, for through your goodness we have received **the bread we offer you**: fruit of the earth and work of human hands, it will become for us the bread of life." Similarly holding the chalice he says: "Blessed are you, Lord God of all creation, for through your goodness we have received **the wine we offer you**: fruit of the vine and work of human hands, it will become our spiritual drink." In these two formulas, the earlier translations "bread to offer" and "wine to offer" are changed to "the bread we offer you" and "the wine we offer you" respectively. While the earlier phrase states the purpose implicitly, the new translation makes it clearer that we are offering bread and wine, fruits of human hands to God. If a parish has custom of singing hymn during the Preparation of the Gifts, one would not even notice these changes. However, the priests are to pay attention to the new words in order to avoid slipping back to the previous wording while saying prayers. After the priest washes his hands, he invites the congregation to pray. The changes in this invitation deserve some mention since they have some deeper theological implications. The new text will read: "Pray brethren, that **my sacrifice and yours** may be acceptable to God, the almighty Father." The previous expression "our sacrifice" is expanded now as "my sacrifice and yours." This change has important pastoral implication. The first letter of St. Peter speaks of holy priesthood and offering spiritual sacrifices acceptable to God through Jesus Christ (I Pet 2:5). Similar thoughts are conveyed in other NT letters as well (Rom 12:1, See also Rom 6:3-4, 13, Phil 2:17). All the baptized members of the congregation join in the one Sacrifice of Mass by uniting the sacrifices of their everyday living in bearing Christian witness in the midst of challenges. This prayer implies that people are not silent spectators during the liturgy but by virtue of their Baptism they join their spiritual sacrifices with the sacrifice offered by the priest in *persona Christi*. The people's response to this prayer will see addition of one word: "May the Lord accept the sacrifice at your hands for the praise and glory of his name, for our good and the good of all his **holy** Church." The word "holy" is added since it is found in the Latin original. The prayer that the priest says at the conclusion of the Preparation of the Gifts includes several textual modifications and additions; hence presupposes attention from the part of the priest and congregation. However there is no change in the people's response "Amen."

3.3.2. The Eucharistic Prayer

The Eucharistic Prayer begins with Preface and concludes with the Doxology. MR 2002 includes several rubrical additions, textual modifications and rearrangements in the prefaces and some Eucharistic prayers for different occasions. Both the priests and people have to be attentive to read the text properly and understand the meaning.

3.3.2.1. Preface

Preface begins with a dialogue between the priest and the people. There are some changes in people's response. We have already explained the significance of the change in the response, "And with your spirit" as response to "The Lord be with you." The chart here below helps to see the difference.

Present Text	Translation from MR 2002
Priest: The Lord be with you.	Priest: The Lord be with you.
All: And **also** with you.	All: **And with your spirit**.
Priest: Lift up your hearts.	Priest: Lift up your hearts.
All: We lift them up to the Lord.	All: We lift them up to the Lord.
Priest: Let us give thanks to the Lord our God.	Priest: Let us give thanks to the Lord our God.
All: It is right **to give him thanks and praise.**	All: **It is right and just**.

The new text is closer to the Latin original. Let us see the significance of these changes

The command Lift up your hearts (*sursum corda*), evokes more than one meaning. Symbolically, God is "on high," and heaven is above earth in spatial analogy.[197] In the liturgical experience, symbolic reality is more emphasized than metaphysical reality.[198] It is an invitation that implies transformation of the community of believers assembled to worship moving beyond their everyday experience to God's presence.[199] To lift our hearts implies offering our lives to God.[200] It is a biblical exhortation in the book of Lamentations (3:41). When the people of the covenant wandered far away from God, they are constantly reminded of the steadfast love of God (*hesed*). The Israelites were exhorted to lift up their hearts to the Lord's presence. This exhortation is accompanied by lifting up one's hands towards heaven in a gesture of prayer on the part of the people (Deut 32:40, Lam 2:19, Ps 63:4, 119:48, 134:2, I Tim 2:8).[201] Heart in liturgical usage means the totality of human life with all its aspirations, inmost mind, and expression of the whole person (Deut 6:5, Mt 22:37). In the Semitic world, heart referred to the whole person with intellect and will.[202]

---

[197] It is a biblical invitation to lift our hearts to the Lord. St. Paul invited the believers to "Set your [their] minds on things that are above..." (Col 3:1-3, See also Eph 2:6).

[198] The thought of heavenly altar is expressed in Christian antiquity (Heb 10:12). St. Irenaeus wrote, "There is then an altar in heaven to which our prayers and our offerings are directed." Cf. *Adversus Haereses* IV, 18,6 in R. Moloney, *Our Eucharistic Prayers in Worship, Preaching and Study*, 116.

[199] That is why this biblical expression has special significance in its use in the context of the Eucharistic prayer.

[200] R. Moloney, *Our Eucharistic Prayers in Worship, Preaching and Study*, 49.

[201] Besides these biblical examples, several ancient Christian arts also acknowledge such gesture in prayer. Cf. "Praying figure in the Catacomb of Domitilla (4th Century)" in Y. Christe, T. Velmans, et al., *Art in the Christian World 300-1500: A Handbook of Styles and Forms* (London: Faber and Faber Ltd., 1982), 39.

[202] J. L. McKenzie, "Aspects of Old Testament Thought," in NJBC, 1295.

Commenting on *Sursum corda,* Cyprian of Carthage said that these words express the mood in which every Christian should properly begin every prayer by suppressing every fleshy and worldly thought and bending the mind solely upon the Lord.[203] For Augustine these words express the Christian attitude: "Our Head is in heaven, and therefore our hearts must also be with him."[204]

With their hearts lifted towards God and entered into sacrificial attitude, the priest then specifies what should be the primary expression of that attitude. It should be one of thankful joy and acceptance of God.[205] The people respond and give their assent: "It is right and just." Through this phrase, three important facts regarding the nature of Christian worship are preserved. First, the thanksgiving is not an isolated prayer of priest but done together with the congregation who join with him in proper response. St. John Chrysostom said, "It is not the priest alone who completes the thanksgiving, but the people with him."[206] Secondly, while it contains many elements from the Jewish liturgy, the Christian liturgy perfects the OT liturgy (Jn 4: 23-24, Heb 4:14, 8: 1ff). Thirdly, the Latin tradition has both juridical and moral overtones that were influenced by Roman thought. For example, the response of the community: "It is right and just" is clearly a Christian expression borrowed from Roman practice. It means the same as the simple Jewish response,

---

[203] Cyprian, *De dom. or.,* c.31. in J. Jungmann, *Mass of the Roman Rite,* vol. 2, 110.

[204] Augustine, *Serm,* 227. in J. Jungmann, *Mass of the Roman Rite,* vol. 2, 110.

[205] We see the biblical reference for this expression in Col 3:1-3, Eph 2:6.

[206] Chrysostom, *In II Cor. hom.,* 18 (PG, 61, 527) in J. Jungmann, *Mass of the Roman Rite,* vol. 2, 111. The preface presents reasons for thanksgiving: the historical events through which Christ has revealed the identity and saving will of God. Cf. F. E. Coady, *Divine Revelation According to the four Eucharistic Prayers of the 1975 Roman Missal* (Rome: Pontificia Universitas Gregoriana, 1994), 81.

"Amen."[207] It endorses the celebrant's intention to formulate and proclaim this prayer of thanksgiving and praise on behalf of the assembly.[208] However, Christian understanding is more than mere juridical expression. Thanksgiving (*eucharistia*) is essentially a Christian activity. St. Paul considered it a way of life: "And be thankful. Let the word of Christ dwell in you richly; teach and admonish one another in all wisdom; and with gratitude in your hearts sing psalms, hymns and spiritual songs to God" (Col 3:15-16). A similar invitation is expressed in his letter to the Ephesians: "...always and for everything giving thanks in the name of our Lord Jesus Christ to God the Father" (Eph 5:20). The new translation adheres to the Latin original which is more a declarative statement than an explanatory sentence.

In the hymn *Sanctus* there is one change in the first sentence. The previous sentence, "Holy, holy, holy Lord God of power and might" is replaced with "Holy, **Holy, H**oly Lord God of **hosts**." The rest of the hymn is unchanged. As one can notice, the word "Holy" is capitalized each time when it is used. During the Arian heresy the Fathers of the Church used the evidence of "Holy, Holy, Holy..." in the liturgy as a witness for Trinitarian interpretation.[209] Adhering to the Latin text, the word "hosts" replaces "power and might" in the previous translation. The word used in the Latin text is *Sabaoth* which is a Hebrew word. Since no equivalent could be found in Latin the Roman Missal has borrowed this Hebrew word in the liturgical use. Though it means "hosts" it refers to the power of God over an army of angels. The word "hosts" means invisible powers which are in force at God's command.

---

[207] In ancient culture such acclamation played important role. It was the proper thing for lawfully assembled people to endorse an important decision, election, taking office, or *leitorgia* (ĕåéôïõñãßá) by means of such public acclamation. Cf. J. Jungmann, *Mass of the Roman Rite*, vol. 2, 111.

[208] L. Soubigou, *A Commentary on the Prefaces*, 9.

[209] The Church at Prayer, vol. 2, 95.

3.3.2.2. Eucharistic Prayers

The new Eucharistic Prayers that were approved after the 1975 Missal are translated and added in the new text which we will soon be using.

3.3.2.2.1. Institution Narrative and Consecration

During the Institution Narrative and Consecration, the Missal repeats the very words of Jesus at the time of Last Supper. Hence when these words are said by the priest, the congregation, assisting deacon, and servers genuflect in adoration. The words said by the priest first holding the bread and then the chalice are changing in the translation.

Present Text	Translation from MR 2002
Take this, all of you, and eat it: this is my body which will be given up for you.Take this, all of you, and drink from it: this is the **cup** of my blood, the blood of the new and **everlasting** covenant. **It** will be **shed** for you and for **all so that sins may be forgiven.** Do this in memory of me.	Take this, all of you, and eat **of** it, **for** this is my body which will be given up for you.Take this, all of you, and drink from it, **for** this is the **chalice** of my blood, the blood of the new and **eternal** covenant, **which** will be **poured out** for you and for **many for the forgiveness of sins.** Do this in memory of me.

As one can notice, the words when the priest holds the bread are not changing much except for insertion of two prepositions "of" and "for." However the words said by priest when he holds the chalice of wine are changing more substantially. The new translation combines several independent clauses with appropriate conjunctions such as "for" and "which" and makes them into one sentence. Besides this combination of clauses the change includes insertion of new words which deserve explanation. The word "chalice" replaces the word "cup." First of all it matches our common way of referring to the sacred vessel at the altar; it draws attention to the ceremonial use of the vessel even at the Last Supper. Besides these two reasons the biblical understanding of the term also supports the use of the term chalice (Ps 23:5, 116:13). The word "everlasting" is replaced by "eternal" referring to the covenant. The word "everlasting" could cause misunderstanding in English, meaning something that lasts for a long period of time. This term may mean that the time is measurable even if it is long. In contrast the term "eternal" which is preferred in the new translation does not have this ambiguity. This term "eternal" is beyond any possible measurement of time. Hence it expresses that the duration of God's covenant with us cannot be measured. The new translation preferred the term "poured" instead of "shed." The word shed could be ambiguous in a sacramental context, where it can be misunderstood as blood shed from a wound on the body of Christ. In contrast the term "poured" is a biblical term used in the context of sacrifice (Gen 35:14, II Kings 16:13, Is 53:12, Mk 14:24). This verb conveys clearly what happened at Calvary where Jesus offered his life as a sacrifice, the sacred commemoration of which is continued at every Holy Mass. Another change in words is "all" being replaced by "many." One has to be clear about two things here: the NT testifies that Jesus came for the salvation of all (Jn 11:52, II Cor 5:14-15, Tit 2:11, I Jn 11:52); nevertheless the word used by Jesus at the Last Supper is translated only as "many" and not "all." The Latin word in the Missal also means "many" and not "all." The phrase "so that sins may be forgiven" is now changed to "for the forgiveness of sins." Though the meaning conveyed in both the phrases is the same, the new translation is precise in emphasis on the reconciling ministry of Jesus. Jesus came not that sins *may* be forgiven, but "for the forgiveness of sins." The new translation is closer to the Latin text.

3.3.2.2.2. The Mystery of Faith

During the Eucharistic Prayer, after the Institution Narrative and Consecration (Elevation), the priest invites the congregation to proclaim the mystery of faith. Until now we are accustomed to hear "Let us proclaim the mystery of faith." Now it is changed to "The mystery of faith." The new phrase is faithful to the Latin original and matches similar structure in the other expressions during Mass such as, "The word of the Lord" and "The gospel of the Lord." The congregation responds to this invitation by saying or singing any one of the three options given in the Missal.[210] This memorial acclamation comes in the midst of a lengthy Eucharistic Prayer where the words of the prayer are directed to God the Father. In the previous translation suddenly the opening of the invitation "Let us" shifts the focus to people, then as the priest continues the prayer, it shifts back to addressing God the Father. The new translation helps to keep the focus intact. The original text in the Latin Missal has only three options for acclamations and the four options that are currently used in the English translation are based on those three Latin texts. The same three acclamations are preserved in the MR 2002; hence three corresponding acclamations are in the new translation. Acclamation is addressed to someone whereas proclamation is made about someone; hence the structure is different. Moreover, in the liturgical tradition, the literary genre of acclamation is prayer and not statement. In the light of these two facts the English translation is revised now. The following chart highlights the changes:

	Present Text	Translation from MR 2002
1.	Dying you destroyed our death, rising you restored our life. Lord Jesus, come in glory.	We proclaim your death, O Lord, and profess your Resurrection until you come again.
2.	When we eat this bread and drink this cup, we proclaim your death, **Lord Jesus**, until you come **in glory.**	When we eat this Bread and drink this Cup, we proclaim your death, **O Lord**, until you come **again.**
3.	**Lord**, by your cross and resurrection you have set us free. **You are the Savior of the world.**	**Save us, Savior of the world, for** by your Cross and Resurrection you have set us free.

---

[210] In the previous English translation there were four options but the Latin original contains only three options for response.

The first acclamation in MR 2002 is very similar to the one that most Catholics are used to: "Christ has died, Christ is risen, Christ will come again." This acclamation in the English Missal used until now is not found in the Latin original, but it was composed based on the first text in the chart. In this familiar acclamation, three intense statements are built without a clear connection, whereas the new translation shows the connection between dying and rising of Christ and also the manner we proclaim it in anticipation of his coming. In the acclamation number two, only the words "O Lord" is changed. The word "O" is inserted for the sake of rhythm. At the end of the acclamation the word "again" is inserted also for rhythm and clarity. In the acclamation number three, the word order is changed. The two titles "Lord" and "Savior" are combined into one "Savior of the world." The various parts of the acclamation are well connected in the new translation and it offers explicit prayer to Jesus. These variations in the new English text also presuppose new music for the same. The choir and the assembly should soon become aware of these changes.

3.3.2.2.3. Doxology

There is a slight change in the doxology at the end of the Eucharistic Prayer. The following chart helps to see the changes.

Present Text	Translation from MR 2002
Through him, with him, in him, in the unity of the Holy Spirit all **glory and honor** is yours almighty Father, for ever and ever.	Through him, **and** with him, **and** in him, **to you, O God, almighty Father**, in the unity of the Holy Spirit, is all **honor and glory**, for ever and ever.

Though the content is the same the new word order follows the Latin flow of words. The new text also clearly expresses that the prayer is offered to God the Father, through Jesus Christ, and in the Holy Spirit.

3.4. The Communion Rite

The Communion Rite refers to the prayers beginning from the Lord's Prayer to Prayer after Communion. There are some minor changes in the words used during this part of the Mass.

3.4.1. Embolism

The Lord's Prayer remains the same, however in the embolism; the prayer said by priest after the Lord's Prayer, there are some changes.

Present Text	Translation from MR 2002
Deliver us, Lord, from every evil, and **grant** us peace in our **day**. In your mercy, keep us free from sin and **protect us from all anxiety** as we wait in **joyful** hope for the coming of our Savior, Jesus Christ.	Deliver us, Lord, **we pray**, from every evil, **graciously** grant peace in our **days, that, by the help of** your mercy, we may be always free from sin and **safe from all distress**, as we await the **blessed** hope and the coming of our Savior, Jesus Christ.

Among the changes highlighted in the chart, two phrases deserve some explanations. First of all, the phrase, "safe from all distress" replaces the previous phrase "protect us from all anxiety." The change is made in order to differentiate circumstances that cause distress from the interior feeling of anxiety. The prayer becomes significant as it prays not only freedom from sin but also protection from all the circumstances that lead to worry. The next change concerns the phrase, "we await the blessed hope and the coming of our Savior, Jesus Christ." This phrase is based on the words of St. Paul in his letter to Titus (2:13). The new translation makes it clear that we await His return even when we do not feel so joyful.

3.4.2. Rite of Peace

After embolism, the priest prays for peace and unity in the Church. This text too has undergone some changes as highlighted in the chart.

Present Text	Translation from MR 2002
Lord Jesus Christ, **you** said to your apostles: **I leave you peace**, my peace I give you. Look not on our sins, but on the faith of your Church, and **grant us** the peace and unity of your kingdom **where you** live for ever and ever.	Lord Jesus Christ, **who** said to your Apostles, **Peace I leave you**, my peace I give you, look not on our sins, but on the faith of your Church, and **graciously grant her** the peace and unity **in accordance with your will. Who** live and reign for ever and ever.

As one can notice, most of the changes are in the word order. The new text uses the pronoun "her" when referring to Church in this prayer. This usage is in line with the Church's image as the bride of Christ. The prayers that follow this prayer for peace do not change except in the "Lamb of God."

3.4.3. Lamb of God

The text for "Lamb of God" includes some changes as shown in the following table.

	Present Text	Translation from MR 2002
Priest	**This is** the Lamb of God who takes away the sins of the world, **Happy** are those **who are called to his supper.**	**Behold** the Lamb of God **behold him** who takes away the sins of the world, **Blessed** are those **called to the supper of the Lamb.**
All	Lord I am not worthy **to receive you,** but only say the word and I shall be healed.	Lord I am not worthy **that you should enter under my roof,** but only say the word and **my soul** shall be healed.

The insertion of the word "Behold" is closer to Latin and sounds more majestic than simple "This." The use of "Behold" maintains allusion to the gospel of John (1:29) where John the Baptist points out Jesus to his followers. The word "Blessed" replaces "Happy," because one can be "Blessed" even when one is in sorrow. The phrase "Supper of the Lamb" is a direct allusion to Revelation 19:9. The change in response, "that you should enter under my roof" is direct link to the gospel account of the Gentile centurion who requested Jesus to heal his servant (Mt 8:8, Lk 7:6). The centurion felt unworthy to have Jesus "enter" his home. Jesus admired his humility and faith and healed the servant from afar. Therefore allusion to this gospel narration reminds us that we are imitating the humility of the centurion so that Jesus will not avoid us because of our sins, but will come to us on account of our surrender in requesting His healing and the strength of our faith. Another change is the word "soul." As a general pattern the previous translation avoided use of the word "soul" throughout the Missal but is now rectified wherever the Latin text meant "soul." In the context of the response we consider here, the specific use of the term "soul" means spiritual healing of forgiveness before receiving the Holy Communion (I Cor 11:27-32).

3.4.4. Prayer after Communion

As there are revisions in the Opening Prayers and other texts of the Mass, soon we will notice new words in the Prayer after Communion said by the priest. Therefore, it requires attention from the priest to read them properly. There is no change in people's response. After this prayer, MR 2002 includes new text known as Prayer over the People (*oratio super populum*) for certain occasions. The theological and liturgical significance of this addition will be discussed in the next chapter. This prayer is said by the priest and there is no people's verbal response.

3.5. Concluding Rite

At the Concluding Rite, there is no change in response except when the congregation responds "And with your spirit" to the invitation "The Lord be with you" before the final blessing. The Missal also gives some new options for dismissal said either by the priest or deacon: "Go forth, the Mass is ended," "Go and announce the Gospel of the Lord," "Go in peace, glorifying the Lord by your life," or "Go in peace." These options are given by recommendation from the synod of bishops of Rome to mean that after the Mass we are not simply leaving the church building but we enter the world with a mission to bear witness through our Christian living.

What we discussed in this chapter is only some examples of noticeable changes in the translation of MR 2002. The MR 2002 is more than simple rearrangement of words and correction of punctuations. There are several textual and rubrical additions, which can be subject of detailed study. Hence, in the next chapter a few examples of these enhanced textual and rubrical modifications will be highlighted.

CHAPTER V
SIGNIFICANT TEXTUAL AND RUBRICAL MODIFICATIONS

MR 2002 is a linear development from the previous Missals as a form of authentic development. The textual and rubrical modifications, new compositions, and corrections are so numerous that we are compelled to examine a limited number of examples and highlights. The vastness of the examination also presupposes a systematic treatment of the changes involved. Hence we will try to study the changes under four sub-titles in this chapter.

1. Changes in the Temporal and the Sanctoral Cycles

The liturgical calendar is divided into two:

- Temporal Cycle, that is, the feasts determined by the events of the life of Christ and the ferias (ordinary days). This cycle includes the liturgical seasons such as Advent, Christmas, Lent, Easter and Ordinary Time.
- Sanctoral Cycle, comprising the feasts of saints plus the common of saints (of martyrs, virgins, and so on).

1.1. Proper of the Time

1.1.1. Advent

The prayers during the Advent that we have in the current Missal are developments from a long tradition that includes a variety of ancient sacramentaries as well as the Missal of 1570, Missal of 1962 and the post-Vatican II Missal of 1970. For example the proper prayers for every day, beginning from December 17 are added for the season of Advent. In the MR 2002 one will see some more changes and new texts. For example the biblical citations for Advent Antiphons are revised according the *Novo Vulgata* (New edition of Vulgate in Latin) published in 1979.[211] The Advent prayers in

---

[211] *Notitae* 15 (1979): 233-235.

MR 2002 can be traced back to *Rotulus* of Ravenna, which contains the oldest liturgical prayers for the days before Christmas. According to the study by S. Benz (*Der Rotulus von Ravenna*, Münster, 1967), these prayers have been composed under the influence of Peter Chrysologus (Bishop of Ravenna, about 432-450). These fifth century prayers reflect the Christological teachings of the Councils of Ephesus (431) and Chalcedon (451).[212] For example, the new Opening Prayer for Mass on December 20 is based on this ancient text.[213] Besides these profound revisions based on the ancient texts, the MR 2002 includes some new additions. For example, the solemn benediction from the Third Sunday of Advent is added in MR 2002. The rubrics are slightly modified to avoid ambiguity in the earlier edition. In general the several prayers used during Advent are retouched to give emphasis on the divine and human natures of Christ. In some prayers the conclusions are changed. For example, the conclusions of the Opening Prayer for December 24 and Prayer over Gifts from December 18-23 are slightly changed to highlight the Christological emphasis.

1.1.2. Christmas Season

During this season the formularies for the vigil of Epiphany are newly composed in MR 2002.[214] Some of the prayers revised during Christmas season are based on the texts found in the Parisian Missal (*Missale Parisiene*),[215] which were originally slightly altered version of Gelasian Sacramentary. Some studies on the sources of the revision and new composition in MR 2002 revealed that these texts are based on the ancient patristic and liturgical sources. For example, the new Prayer over Gifts for Epiphany is based on the

---

[212] A. Rose, "Les oraisons du Rotulus de Ravenne," QL 4 (1971): 271-294. See also M. E. Johnson, *Between Memory and Hope*, 362.

[213] MR 2002, 145. See also M. Barba, *Il Messale Romano*, 52.

[214] MR 2002, 173-174. See also A. Lameri, *Tempo di Avvento e di Natale*, in *Rivista Liturgica* 90 (2003): 593-594.

[215] M. Barba, *Il Messale Romano*, 53.

Sermon of St. Augustine[216] and *Rotulus* of Ravenna.[217] The Post-Communion prayer is a revised version from the Gelasian Sacramentary. The rubrical revision has made clear the use of the Gloria every day during the Christmas season. In general these additions and modifications have enriched and clarified the text of MR 2002.

1.1.3. Lent

During the season of Lent two additions can be seen in MR 2002: rubrics for the Sundays of Lent and Prayer over the People (*oratio super populum*). The rubrics at the beginning of Lent make clear the two Lenten motifs: penitential and baptismal. The rubrics also highlight the communal aspect of penance. The rubrical additions and clarifications make a better connection between the baptismal motif of the Lenten season and the Ritual Mass for the Rite of Christian Initiation. The rubrics for the first, the second and the third scrutinies make this connection in unambiguous terms. The Prayer over People at the end of the Mass was an ancient custom and this prayer is found in several ancient sacramentaries such as Gelasian and several other Roman Missals. This prayer was omitted in the Tridentine Missal and the Missal of 1970. The ancient practice is restored in MR 2002.[218] The Opening Prayer and Prayer over Gifts on the Saturday of the Fifth week were redundant; hence they are completely revised based on the text in Gelasian.[219] This new Opening Prayer brings out Mary's role in the passion of Christ.[220]

1.1.3.1. Holy Week

The rubrical changes emphasize the preparation for the celebration of Paschal Mystery, the important and central feast for

---

[216] Augustine, *Sermo,* 204, 2 in PL 38, 1037.

[217] S. Benz, *Der Rotulus von Ravenna* (Münster, 1967), 265-273.

[218] M. Barba, *Il Messale Romano,* 57.

[219] Ibid, 58-59.

[220] MR 2002, 265.

Christians. The rubrics have been clarified for the Chrism Mass and the Mass of the Lord's Supper on the Holy Thursday. All the biblical references during the Holy Week liturgy are revised according the *Novo Vulgata* 1979. The texts as well as the rubrics address several important aspects of Holy Week which are so fundamental to the life of the Church.

1.1.3.2. Easter Triduum

In the liturgy for the Easter Triduum, MR 2002 introduces new formulary for the Mass of the Lord's Supper in the Roman Canon.[221] The rubrics make a distinction between the celebrations at a cathedral or parish church. In the Good Friday liturgy during the General Intercessions, appropriate changes are made in petition number three for bishops[222] corresponding to GIRM 149. During the Paschal vigil the solemn blessing by the bishop is revised according to the Ceremonial for Bishops.

1.1.4. Paschal Season

The institution of the feast of Divine Mercy on the Second Sunday of Easter required new prayers in MR 2002.[223] This feast was introduced in response to requests that came from many parts of the world. The introduction of new formularies during the octave of Ascension is based on Parisian Missal of 1738.[224] A new rubric is introduced for the liturgy on the Wednesday of the sixth week of Easter. There are several minor modifications in the prayers said on the following days during Easter season: Monday, Thursday, Friday and Saturday of the second week, Mondays of the third and the fourth weeks, Saturday of the fourth week, Fifth Sunday, Monday of the fifth week, and Tuesday of the sixth week. All these prayers

---

[221] MR 2002, 305-311.

[222] MR 2002, 317.

[223] MR 2002, 386. See also *Notitiae* 31 (1995): 16-18.

[224] MP 1738, 1493. See also M. Barba, *Il Messale Romano*, 69.

mostly Opening Prayers are revised and retouched based on the ancient sacramentaries such as Hadrianum, Gregorian and Gelasian.

1.1.5. Ordinary Time

During the Ordinary Time there are no major changes either in the texts or structure, except some minor textual and rubrical changes. For example the Opening Prayer of eighteenth Sunday is retouched according to the original manuscripts of Veronese Sacramentary based on which it was written. Similarly the Opening Prayer on nineteenth Sunday is also revised based on the original manuscripts of Gregorian and Padunese Sacramentaries.

1.2. Order of the Mass

In the Order of the Mass there are no changes except some rubrical clarifications and some minor changes in the Rite of Blessing of water. There are some slight modifications in the solemn blessing during the Masses on the following occasions: Nativity of the Lord, Holy Spirit, Blessed Virgin Mary and All Saints.[225]

1.3. Proper of Saints

The main change in the Sanctoral section of MR 2002 is addition of newly canonized saints after the promulgation of the previous Missal of 1975. There are eight such new saints introduced in the universal calendar: Adalbert (23 April), Ludovici Mariae Grignion of Monfort (28 April), Peter Juliani Eymard (2 August), Maximilian Maria Kolbe (14 August), Peter Claver (9 September), Andrew Kim Taegon (20 September), Laurentii Ruiz (28 September), and Andrew Dung-Lac (24 November). New formularies for the following optional memorial celebrations are introduced in MR 2002: Name of Jesus (Jan 3), Josephine Bakhita, virgin (Feb 8), Our Lady of Fatima (May 13), Christopher Magallanes, priest and martyr (May 21), Rita of Cascia, religious (May 22), Augustine Zhao Rong, priest and martyr (July 9), Apollinaris, bishop and martyr (July 20), Sarbelii

---

[225] M. Barba, *Il Messale Romano*, 81-83.

Makhluf, priest (July 24), Therese of the Blessed Cross, virgin and martyr (Aug 9), Name of Mary (Sept 12), and Catherine of Alexandria, virgin and martyr (Nov 25). New prayers for saints from different geographical territories are introduced in the universal calendar and new formularies are added in MR 2002: Paul Miki and companions, martyrs in Japan, Christopher Magallanes and companions, martyrs in Mexico, Charles Lwanga and companions, martyrs in Uganda, Augustine Zhao Rong and companions, martyrs in China, Andrew Kim Taegon, martyrs in Korea, Laurenti Ruiz and companions, martyrs in Philippinnes, John Brebeuf and Isaac Jogues, martyrs in Canada, and Andrew Dung-Lac and companions, martyrs in Vietnam. The prayers used on the feast days of some saints have been retouched. In some instances certain new formularies are added. For example the prayers for the celebration of Athanaisus, Philip Neri, Irenaeus, Benedict, Bernard, Leo the Great, Francis Xavier, and Ambrose did not have proper antiphons in the Missal of 1975. The rubrics mention that one of the antiphons from the Common of Saints can be chosen for these celebrations. MR 2002 has introduced new antiphons for the formularies used on the feast day of these saints. These examples of the revision in the sanctoral prove how the new prayers and changes in MR 2002 has enhanced the prayers used on the feast, memorial or optional memorial of these saints.

2. Prayer over the People

Prayer over the People refers to the set of prayers said after the Post Communion Prayers. In the ancient sacramentaries such as Milanese and Veronese, these prayers received importance next to preface, because they sum up the theme of the liturgy of that day or season before people leave the church after the final blessing. The Gregorian Sacramentary and the Post-Tridentine Missal preserved these prayers for several days during the liturgical year. Especially in the Gregorian Sacramentary the Prayer over the People during Lent received greater significance because the prayer highlighted the Lenten character. The Gelasian also gave importance to this prayer especially during Christmas, Lent and Easter seasons. Although the Missal of 1570 retained some of these prayers, the prayers over the people meant for Lent were omitted. During the liturgical reform after Vatican II, the unique character and structure of this prayer had not been deeply studied, except the studies done by *Cœtus*, the study group responsible for revision of various parts of the Mass under the direction of the Concilium. As a result, the Missal of 1970 retained only some Prayers over the People on Sundays. On the other hand, taking advantage of subsequent studies on this prayer, understanding the significance of these prayers and following the model of ancient sacramentaries, the MR 2002 has included Prayer over the People for many occasions through out the liturgical year. In the Missal each set of prayers such as Opening Prayers, Prayer over Gifts and Post-Communion has a specific structure. Similarly the Prayer over the People also has a unique structure. In the Opening Prayer the priest says the prayer on behalf of the community. When the priest uses the expression "our prayer" he includes himself in the Opening Prayer. In contrast, during the Prayer over the People, the expressions such as "their prayer," "your family" or "your people" are used. In this prayer priest is not part of it, but he plays an intermediary role which is made clear by these different expressions. The object of this prayer is people; hence the title Prayer over the People (*oratio super populum*).[226]

3. Mary in the Paschal Mystery

Mary's role in the history of salvation has long been acknowledged in the Tradition of the Church and several Marian chants and prayers during liturgy testify to this fact. The foundation for this practice is Christological and rooted in the Mystery of Incarnation.[227]

---

[226] M. Barba, *Il Messale Romano*, 118-121.
[227] Ibid, 181.

3.1. Medieval Practices

Several medieval Missals highlighted Mary's contemplation of Calvary, while Jesus was showing His love for humanity. The sorrowful mother who wept at the foot of the Cross, cried not only for her son who was hanging on the Cross, but also for the entire humanity. Based on this reflection several pious devotions connected with Mary began during Lent. Besides the popular devotions the Missal also had chants that emphasized the same reflection (e.g. Stabat Mater). The sacred commemoration of the supreme sacrifice of Jesus during liturgy was further cherished through popular devotions.

3.2. Studies on Marian Prayers

During the period before and after Vatican II several studies were done on various aspects of Marian prayers in the liturgy: P. Jounel studied the prayers for the feasts of Mary in the Roman liturgical calendar, F. Brovelli studied the memorials of Mary in the Roman Missal, W. Beninert studied Marian devotions from theological, liturgical and pastoral perspectives, and A. Augé studied celebration of Mary in the Mystery of Christ.[228] In 1974 the publication of *Marialis cultus*[229] stimulated new avenues to study the role Mary in the salvation as highlighted in the liturgy,[230] which also underlined the theological value of such devotions flowing from liturgy.

3.3. Revision of Marian Prayers in MR 2002

MR 2002 has incorporated these theological values of Mary's role in the salvation in its prayers and chants. However MR 2002 is careful that the emphasis on Mary's role in the salvation should not

---

[228] M. Barba, *Il Messale Romano*, 178-179.

[229] *Marialis cultus* 16-23, in AAS 66 (1974): 128-134.

[230] A. M. Tricca, *Esemplarità della presenza di Maria SS. Nella celebrazione del mistero di Cristo* in EL 102 (1988): 406-435.

obscure the primary focus on the Paschal Mystery, but should only enhance it.

MR 2002 has many additions especially Opening Prayers that focus on the Mary's role in the redemption following the idea of Mary as co-redeemer. Some of the themes include: Holy Mary, the disciple of the Lord; Blessed Virgin Mary at the Cross; Commendation of Blessed Virgin Mary; Blessed Virgin Mary, Mother of Reconciliation; Blessed Virgin Mary in the Lord's Resurrection; Holy Mary, source of light and life; and Blessed Virgin Mary, Queen of Apostles. Most of the changes in the Opening Prayers occur during the Lent[231] and Easter seasons.[232] These changes go hand in hand with the prayers in the Liturgy of the Hours. Most of the new Marian Prayers in MR 2002 are from the collection of prayers already approved by the Congregation for Divine Worship on the occasion of the Marian Year (1987-1988) and promulgated by John Paul II.

4. Mass for the Dead

MR 2002 has included some new prayers in the Mass for the Dead. The number of prayers has been increased from 114 to 120 based on a thorough study of various biblical, patristic, magisterial and liturgical texts. Though the 1970 Missal enhanced the content of the prayer based on similar sources,[233] there were still some inconsistencies which are rectified in the MR 2002. For example the post-communion prayer outside Easter season-A which prays in order that the sacrament of Christ's body and blood may guide us on our pilgrim way to your kingdom, is based on the sermon of St. Peter Chrysologus.[234] The Opening Prayer outside Easter season that prays for God's mercy and the joy of saints is based on the

---

[231] e.g. Opening Prayer on Friday during fifth week of Lent MR 2002, 265.

[232] M. Barba, *Il Messale Romano*, 189.

[233] H. Ashworth, "The Prayers for the Dead in the Missal of Pope Paul VI," EL 85 (1971): 3-15.

[234] Peter Chrysologus, *Sermo* 68 in PL 52, 395C. See MR 2002, 1192.

Gregorian Sacramentary.[235] Several studies on the sources of these prayers linked the present text to Veronese, Gelasian and Gregorian Sacramentaries.[236] MR 2002 has retouched these prayers corresponding to these liturgical and patristic sources.

MR 2002 has returned to use of the word *anima* which means "soul" in harmony with the old Tradition. The previous editions of the post-Vatican II missals were inconsistent in the use of this term and in many instances the expression "eternal life" was used instead of the term "soul." Already in 1979, some concerns were raised by the Congregation for the Doctrine of Faith, about the issue of the inconsistent use of the word *anima* and the ambiguity it may cause in understanding anthropology and eschatology[237]. Homogeneous use of the word in MR 2002 has clarified the theology and has avoided possible misunderstanding of Church's teachings on anthropology and eschatology. MR 2002 has restored the word *anima* in thirty prayers.[238]

In this chapter we have only introduced the some examples of changes and their theological and liturgical significance. There are many other changes like the textual variations in the Opening Prayers for the eighteen Sundays of Ordinary Time, the clarity made with regard to the use of the terms creation and redemption, textual alterations in the prayers for the Common of Saints, and addition of antiphons. For further examination of any particular aspect of the change one may refer to the sources indicated in the footnotes. As these examples reveal, MR 2002 is certainly enhanced in content with theological clarity and it is the desire of the Church that this new edition of the Roman Missal and its translation in vernacular would assist the faithful to fruitful celebration of the Eucharist and promote authentic ongoing liturgical renewal in the Church.

---

[235] MR 2002, 1192 (C).

[236] M. Barba, *Il Messale Romano*, 322-282.

[237] AAS 71 (1979): 940-941.

[238] For more examples of the restoration and their sources in ancient Sacramentaries see M. Barba, *Il Messale Romano*, 394-410.

CHAPTER VI

SCHEMA FOR LITURGICAL CATECHESIS

MR 2002 will be instrumental for more efficient liturgical renewal if proper catechesis precedes the introduction of its translation to the vernacular. A systematic preparation for the introduction of MR 2002 will prepare people for full and active participation in the liturgy. A serious knowledge of the meaning of the prayers in the Roman Missal constitutes an important aspect of the liturgical catechesis. Without such serious knowledge there is always a possibility that our actions may turn into hallow ritualism without its actualization in life. At the same time, catechesis should not be only an intellectual exercise failing to come alive in liturgical practice.[239] One must balance these two aspects in liturgical catechesis. From these two, flows the third aspect in liturgical catechesis. That is, what one learns in a systematic catechesis must lead to transformation of life.[240] This transformation must lead to discipleship by living the Paschal mystery we celebrate in the liturgy.[241] In order to have a systematic liturgical catechesis I propose three steps which I hope may be useful in parishes.

Step 1. Know the Missal

The knowledge of the Missal prayers does not simply mean familiarizing the sections that we will be using during the daily liturgy. The Roman Missal is not just one book that we pull out of a stack of books and begin to use it, but the Missal has to be understood in the

---

[239] *National Directory for Catechesis* (Washington, DC: USCCB, 2005), #33.

[240] Systematic catechesis, which is a cognitive domain of general education, must lead to transformation or conversion of life, which is affective domain.

[241] The discipleship is the behavioral domain. Cf. J. Mondoy, "Liturgy Education in the Curriculum," *Liturgical Ministry* (Winter 2009): 27.

proper context of the Tradition of the Church in order to appreciate the meaning of its prayers. The Roman Missal is connected with the ancient as well as recent sources due to the theological and liturgical significance.

Liturgical texts evolve in specific historical and theological contexts; hence, any attempt to study liturgical books presupposes background study of the text before the actual examination of the text. That is why Cyrille Vogel and Henry Ashworth[242] have insisted upon the historical context in understanding the Roman Missal. For example, Cyrille emphasizes two aspects in understanding of the euchological texts:[243] the chronological and geographical coordination of the manuscripts;[244] and their archetypes in a variety of texts of the same tradition.[245] Henry Ashworth also emphasizes the same, because for him such examination will assist the researcher to understand the extent the antecedent liturgical sources have influenced the present text.[246]

In order to facilitate increased participation among believers in learning the richness of the Missal prayers and the Holy Mass, seminars, workshops and input sessions may be organized at diocesan

---

[242] These two are well-known researchers in liturgical scholarship. Henry was member in the *Cœtus* XIIIbis, the commission that was responsible for the revision of new prefaces in the post Vatican II missal.

[243] C. Vogel, *Medieval Liturgy*, 62-63.

[244] This coordination is necessary since the manuscripts were copied and preserved not merely for the sake of preservation but only because they were actually used in the liturgies of that period.

[245] Examining the sources of the liturgical texts is important because in the Middle Ages, "pure manuscripts" as such did not exist, but they were the results of ritual cross-fertilization and products of a very long process. When the newer and more developed texts were introduced, they did not set aside the earlier or less evolved texts. Cf. C. Vogel, 62-63.

[246] H. Ashworth, "Some Missal Prayers in the light of Pauline Theology," *Liturgy*, 32 (1963): 37.

and parish levels with a team of personnel who are knowledgeable and give correct interpretation according to Church teaching. It is important that such sessions are conducted for priests, persons involved in various liturgical ministries, and the lay faithful. These instructions must take place several months before the introduction of the translation so that each one concerned will have time to reflect on the richness of the Missal prayers and interiorize them.

Step 2. Contemplative-Communication

The second step we call "contemplative-communication," is composed of three elements: communication, contemplation and openness. In this book, communication refers to the Word of God enshrined in liturgy,[247] because *Dei Verbum* uses the Latin verb *communicare*[248] to describe God's revelation and points out that "the sacred liturgy ...is full of the divine word."[249] Similarly Pope Benedict XVI calls "the Liturgy, privileged setting for the word of God."[250] This divine word in liturgy can be rightly understood and interpreted only within the Tradition of the Church. Therefore, it is not sufficient to *look* at the liturgy for the words from Scripture, but one must be *engaged* with it by contemplating the mystery in the

---

[247] Cypriano Vagaggini emphasized that the liturgy serves as an admirable mirror in which is reflected and summed up the entirety of God's revelation to humans; it is the projection into the present of the whole history of salvation, past, present and future. Cf. C. Vagaggini, *Initiation theologique a la liturgie*, vol. 1, 73 in "The Christology of the Roman Missal" *Historical and Theological Aspects of the Roman Missal*, 17.

[248] DV #6 in Flannery, 99-100.

[249] DV #25 in Flannery, 113-114.

[250] *Verbum Domini*, #52.

act of prayer.[251] This contemplation[252] is necessary to interiorize the Word present in liturgy.[253] That is why our step is also described as "contemplative." The contents of faith can be grasped only through engagement with the communication in the liturgy and not by a detached observation. For this reason contemplation - though understood as solitary reflection in ordinary sense - becomes important in our understanding of liturgical texts.

The spiritual engagement with the text presupposes openness, allowing the divine word to penetrate the human experience of understanding. This aspect is specifically important for our proposed step in the context of initial fear and discomfort at the introduction of the translation of the new edition of the Roman Missal. A specifically *contemplative* approach in our step disarms our prejudices and allows us to consider each text without polemic or

---

[251] That is why Hans Urs Von Balthasar insisted that Theology should be done on one's knees. Cf. E. Oakes, *Pattern of Redemption: Theology of Hans Urs von Balthasar* (New York: Continuum, 1994), 7.

[252] Mahatma Gandhi once said that there are three types of creatures in the universe. The living creatures living deep in the sea which are silent, the birds of the air singing and making joyful sounds, and the creatures on earth among which the animals scream or roar but only man is capable of all the three. He has the depth of sea, burden of earth and joy of heaven. Cardinal Ratzinger adds to this writing of Gandhi by pointing out how liturgy is cosmic in character, for it sings with angels, silent with the depths of universe and redeems from the burdens of earth. Cf. M. F. Mannion, *Masterworks of God: Essays in Liturgical Theory and Practice* (Mundelein, IL: Hillenbrand Books, 2004), 189-190. Among the three categories of species, only man is capable of contemplation as the steward of all creation (Gen 1). In his contemplation, he leads the whole creation to God by offering praise and thanksgiving in worship (Rom 8:18-23).

[253] This divine-human communication is actualized in the "contemplation and study of believers who ponder these things in their hearts (Lk 2:19,51)." The writings of the Fathers of the Church are a witness for this "life-giving presence" of divine revelation in "the believing and praying Church." Cf. DV #8 in Flannery, 102.

politic. It is an approach based on reflection rather than reaction. It allows us to see the allusions from Scripture in the words and phrases of the liturgical text. The divine word proclaimed and the vivid memories of the history of salvation commemorated in the Mass make a lasting impression on believers. The Church partakes of the bread of life "from the one table of the Word of God and the Body of Christ."[254] Although the liturgical texts may not quote them directly, the revelation in Scripture finds a ritual voice in the Prayer of the Church. Throughout the centuries liturgy has grown and developed, yet has remained faithful to its foundation in Scripture. The liturgy assimilates the wealth of Tradition and employs the scriptures for the spiritual nourishment of God's people.[255] In order to effectively engage in the contemplation of the prayers from the Roman Missal one may find it useful to follow the four steps of Lectio Divina: *lectio* (reading), *meditatio* (reflection/rumination), *oratio* (prayer), and *contemplatio* (contemplation).[256] Priests and lay faithful may begin to read the Missal prayers as a part of their personal meditation and interiorize the rich content of the expressions. Such spiritual familiarization before the celebration of Holy Mass will enhance one's active participation during the liturgy.

Step 3. Celebration of Liturgy

A serious knowledge gained through reading, seminars, and workshops organized at parish/diocesan levels together with personal spiritual interiorization of the Missal prayers must then lead to full

---

[254] DV # 21, in Flannery, 111-112. Hence, one can expect to find scriptures present in some way in the Prayer of the Church. Cf. F. E. Coady, *Divine Revelation According to the four Eucharistic Prayers*, 18.

[255] F. E. Coady, *Divine Revelation According to the four Eucharistic Prayers*, 7.

[256] M. Magrassi, *Praying the Bible: An Introduction to Lectio Divina*, trans. E. Hagman (Collegeville, MN.: The Liturgical Press, 1998), 103-119. See also M. B. Pennington, *Lectio Divina: Renewing the Ancient Practice of praying for Scripture* (New York: Crossroad Publishing Company, 1998).

and active participation in the liturgy; hence liturgical catechesis should spring from liturgy itself. In the third step priests can make use of the homilies to explain the theological significance of the Missal prayers and assist the congregation to find profound meaning in the celebration. Various ministers in the liturgy such as deacons, acolytes, lectors, choir and others have important roles to help the congregation in a meaningful celebration of the liturgy. For example the MR 2002 clarifies the roles of the ministers and following them appropriately enhances orderly liturgy. Since some expressions in the Gloria, Creed and Sanctus are changed in English, the choir with good practice can beautifully lead the congregation singing the hymns during liturgy. A proper coordination of these ministries helps the congregation to appreciate the rich content of the Missal prayers.

BIBLIOGRAPHY

Roman Missals

Missale Romanum (1570): Editio Princeps. Libreria Editrice Vaticana, 1998.

Missale Romanum (1962). Libreria Editrice Vaticana, 2007.

Missale Romanum: Editio Typica. Libreria Editrice Vaticana, 1970.

Missale Romanum: Editio Typica Altera. Libreria Editrice Vaticana, 1975.

Missale Romanum: Editio Typica Tertia. Libreria Editrice Vaticana, 2002.

Council Documents

Sacrosanctum Concilium Oecumenicum Vaticanum II. *AAS* 58 (1966).

_____. "Dei Verbum." *AAS* 58 (1966): 817-35.

_____. "Sacrosanctum Concilium." *AAS* 56 (1964): 97-138.

Tanner, N. P., ed. *Decrees of the Ecumenical Councils.* With Latin and English Texts. 2 Volumes. London: Shed & Ward Ltd, 1990.

Critical Editions

Bannister, H. M., ed. *Missale Gothicum: A Gallican Sacramentary.* HBS 52 & 54. London: Harrison, 1917-1919.

Botte, B. *La Tradition apostolique de Saint Hippolyte.* Liturgiewissenschaftliche Quellen und Forschungen 39. Münster: Aschendorffsche Verlagsbuchhandlung, 1989

Bradshaw, P. F. et.al., *The Apostolic Tradition.* Minneapolis, MN.: Fortress Press, 2002

Deshusses, J., ed. *Le Sacramentaire Grégorien: Ses principales formes d'apres les plus anciens manuscrits.* 2 vols. E éd. Spicilegium Friburgense, 16 & 24. Fribourg (Suisse): Editions Universitaires, 1971-1979.

Dumas, A. and J. Deshusses., eds. *Liber Sacramentorum Gellonensis.* 2 vols. CC, ser. Catina, 159-159a. Turnhout: Brepols, 1981.

Feltoe, C. L., ed. *Sacramentarium Leonianum.* Cambridge: Cambridge University Press, 1896.

Gamber, K., ed. *Sacramentarium Gregorianum.* 2 vols. Textus patristici et liturgici, 4 et 6. Regensburg: Pustet, 1966-1967.

Moeller, E. *Corpus Præfationum.* vol.161A, IX-X. *Corpus Christianorum Series Latina* 161. Turnholti : Brepols, 1981.

_____. *Corpus Orationum.* vol. 1 ff. *Corpus Christianorum Series Latina* 160. Turnholti : Brepols, 1991.

Mohlberg, C., ed. *Missale Gallicanum Vetus.* Rerum Ecclesiasticarum Documenta, 3. Rome: Herder, 1958.

_____. *Sacramentarium Veronense.* Rerum Ecclesiasticarum Documenta, 1. Rome: Herder, 1956.

Moreton, B. *The Eighth century Gelasian Sacramentary: A Study in Tradition.* London: Oxford University Press, 1976.

Paredi, A., ed. *Saramentarium Bergomense: Maoscritto del secolo IX della Biblioteca dis.* Alessandro in Colonna in Bergamo. MB. 6. Bergamo: Edizioni "monumenta Bergomensio," 1962.

Wilson, H. A., ed. *The Gregorian Sacramentary under Charles the Great.* Henry Bradshaw Society Publications, 49. London: Harrison 1915.

_____. *The Gelasian Sacramentary.* Oxford: Clarendon Press, 1894.

Translations

Abbott, W. M. and J. Gallagher., ed. *The Documents of Vatican II.* New York: Crossroad, 1989.

Bugnini, A. *The Reform of the Liturgy 1948-1975.* Translated by. Matthew J. O'Connell. Collegeville, MN.: The Liturgical Press, 1983.

Carlen, C. *Papal Pronouncements.* 5 Volumes. Ann Arbor, MI.: The Pierian Press, 1981.

Congregation for Divine Worship and Discipline of Sacraments, *Liturgiam Authenticam: Fifth instruction on Vernacular Translation of the Roman Liturgy.* Washington, DC.: USCCB, 2001.

Documents on the Liturgy 1963 – 1979: Conciliar, Papal and Curial Texts. Collegeville, MN.: The Liturgical Press, 1982.

Works On Missal

Books

Adam, A. *The Eucharistic Celebration, the Source and Summit of Faith.* Collegeville, Minnesota: The Liturgical Press, 1994.

Barba, M. *Il Messale Romano: Tradizione e Progresso nella terza editzione tipica.* Città del Vaticano: Libreria Editrice Vaticana, 2004.

Botte, B. *Le Canon de la Messe Romaine.* Louvain: Abbaye du Mont César, 1935.

_____. *Le Mouvement Liturgique: Témoniage et souvenirs.* Paris: Desclée, 1973.

_____. Les traductions liturgiques de l'écriture. "La parole dans la liturgie" 48 *Lex orandi.* Paris: Les editions du cerf, 1970. Pg. 81-105.

_____ and Christine Mohramann. *L'Ordinaire de la Messe.* Paris: Cerf, 1953.

Bouyer, L. "The different forms of Eucharistic Prayer and their Genealogy." *Studia Patristica.* vol. 8., ed. F. L. Cross. *Texte und untersuchungen zur geschichte der altchristlichen literatur,* 93. Berlin: Akademia-Verlag, 1966.

_____. *Eucharist: Theology and Spirituality of the Eucharistic Prayer.* Notre Dame, IN: University of Notre Dame Press, 1968.

_____. *The Liturgy Revived: A Doctrinal Commentary of the Conciliar Constitution on the Liturgy.* South Bend: Notre Dame Press, 1964.

Brun, P. L. "Explication de la messe," *Lex Orandi* 9. Paris: Les éditions du cerf, 1949.

Bruylants, P. *Les Oraisons du Missel Romain.* Vol. 1 & 2. Louvain: Abbaye du Mont César, 1952.

Chupungco, A. J. *Handbook for Liturgical Studies.* Collegeville, MN.: Liturgical Press, 1997. vol. 3 and 4.

Croegaert, A. *The Mass: A Liturgical Commentary,* vol. 1 and 2. Westminster, MD.: The Newman Press, 1959.

Deiss, L. *Springtime of the Liturgy: Liturgical Texts of the First Four Centuries.* Translated by Matthew J. O'Connell. Collegeville, MN.: The Liturgical Press, 1979.

_____., ed. *Early Sources of the Liturgy.* Translated by Benet Weatherhead. London: Geoffrey Chapman, 1967.

Dix, G. *The Shape of the Liturgy.* London: A & C Black, 1986.

Ellard, G. *Master Alcuin, Liturgist: A Partner of Our Piety.* Chicago: Loyola University Press, 1956.

Foley, E, N. D. Mitchell, and J. M. Pierce. *A Commentary on the General Instruction of the Roman Missal.* With Latin and English texts of the Instruction. Collegeville, MN.: Liturgical Press, 2007.

Gy, P. M. *The Reception of Vatican II: Liturgical Reforms in the Life of the Church.* Milwaukee, WI.: Marquette University Press, 2003.

Irwin, K. "The Constitution on the Sacred Liturgy, *Sacrosanctum Concilium* (4 December, 1963)." In *Vatican II and its Documents: An American Reappraisal.,* ed. Timothy O'Connell, 9-38. Wilmington: Michael Glazier, 1986.

Jounel, P. *Les premières étapes de la réforme liturgiques.* 3 volumes. Paris: Desclée, 1965.

Jungmann, J. A. *The Mass of the Roman Rite: Its origins and Development.* Translated by Francis A. Brunner. 2 volumes. Allen, Texas: Christian Classics, 1950.

_____. "Constitution on the Sacred Liturgy." In *Commentary on the Documents of Vatican II.,* ed. Herbert Vorgrimler, vol. 1, 1-88. London: Burns and Oates, 1966.

Klauser, T. *A Short History of the Western Liturgy.* Translated by John Halliburton. London: Oxford University Press, 1969.

Lionel, J. *Speak O Lord.* Bangalore, India: Asian Trading Corporation, 2006.

_____. *Let us Celebrate.* Bangalore, India: Asian Trading Corporation, 2006.

Martimort, A. G., ed. *The Church at Prayer: The Eucharist.* vol. 2. Translated by Matthew J. O'Connell. Shannon, Ireland: Irish University Press, 1973.

_____. *The Church at Prayer: The Introduction to Liturgy.* vol. 1. Translated by Matthew J. O'Connell. Shannon, Ireland: Irish University Press, 1973.

_____. *The Church at Prayer: The Liturgy and Time.* vol. 4. Translated by Matthew J. O'Connell. Shannon, Ireland: Irish University Press, 1973.

Mazza, E. *Eucharistic Prayers of the Roman Rite.* Translated by Matthew J. O'Connell. New York: Pueblo Publications Company, 1986.

_____.*The Origins of the Eucharistic Prayer.* Translated by R. E. Lane (Collegeville, MN.: The Liturgical Press, 1995

_____. *Mystagogy: A Theology of Liturgy in the Patristic Age.* Translated by Matthew J. O'Connell. New York: Pueblo Publishing Company, 1989.

Metzger, M. *History of the Liturgy: The Major Stages.* Translated by Madeleine Beaumont. Collegeville, MN.: The Liturgical Press, 1997.

Nocent, A. *La celebration eucharistique avant et après Saint Pie V.* Le pointe théologique 23. Paris: Beauchesne, 1977.

Oury, G. M. *La messe de Saint Pie V à Paul VI.* Solesmes: Abbaye Saint Pierre, 1975.

Palazzo, É. *A History of Liturgical Books.* Translated by M. Beaumont. Collegeville, MN.: The Liturgical Press, 1998.

Peckers, K. *The Genius of the Roman Rite: On the Reception and Implementation of the New Missal.* Collegeville, MN.: Liturgical Press, 2009.

Ratzinger, J. *The Spirit of the Liturgy.* San Francisco: Ignatius Press, 2000.

_____. *The Feast of Faith: Approaches to a Theology of the Liturgy.* Translated by G. Harrison. San Francisco: Ignatius Press, 1986.

Reid, A., ed. *Looking Again at the Question of Liturgy with Cardinal Ratzinger: Proceedings of the July 2001 Fontgombault Liturgical Conference.* Farnborough: St. Michael Abbey, 2003.

_____. *The Organic Development of the Liturgy.* Farnborough: St. Michael Abbey, 2004.

Sacred Liturgy of the Second Vatican Council. With commentary by Gerard S. Sloyan. Glen Rock, NJ: Paulist Press, 1964.

Theological and Historical Aspects of the Roman Missal: The proceedings of the Fifth International Colloquium of Historical, Canonical and Theological studies on the Roman Catholic liturgy. Kingston and Surbiton, UK: CIEL, 2000.

Vagaggini, C. *The Canon of the Mass and Liturgical Reform.* Translated by Peter Coughlin. New York: Alba House, 1967.

_____. *Theological Dimensions of the Liturgy.* Translated by Leonard J. Doyle. Collegeville, MN.: Liturgical Press, 1959.

Vogel, C. *Medieval Liturgy: An Introduction to the Sources.* Translated by William G. Storey and Niels Krogh Rasmussen. Washington, D.C.: The Pastoral Press, 1981.

Articles

Ashworth, H. "Les sources patristiques du nouveau missel romain." *Questions liturgiques* 4 (1971): 295-304.

_____ . "Some Missal Prayers in the light of Pauline Theology." *Liturgy* 32 (1963): 37.

_____ . "The Liturgical prayers of St. Gregory the Great." *Traditio* 15 (1959): 107-161.

Botte, B. "La prière du célébrant." *La Maison-Dieu* 20 (1950): 133-152.

Bugnini, A. "Pius XII et liturgia." *Ephemerides Liturgicae* 72 (1958): 375-383.

Cabie, R. "Le nouvel 'ordo missae.'" *La Maison-Dieu* 100 (1969): 21-35.

Dumas, A. "Les sources du nouveau missel romain." *Notitae* 7 (1971): 37-42, 74-77, 94-95, 134-136, 276-280.

_____ . "Les oraisons du nouveau missel romain." *Questions Liturgiques* 4 (1971): 263-270.

Gy, P. M. "La réforme liturgique de Trente et celle de Vatican II." *La Maison-Dieu* 128 (1976): 61-75.

_____. "L'unification liturgique de l'occident, et la liturgie de la curie romaine." *Revue des sciences philosophiques et theologiques* 59 (1975): 601-612.

Jounel, P. "Le nouveau propre de France," *La Maison-Dieu* 72 (1962): 141-165.

_____. "Les sources françaises du missel de Paul VI," *Questions Liturgicæ* 4 (1971): 305-316.

Pristas, L. "Theological Principles That Guided the Redaction of the Roman Missal (1970)." *The Thomist* 67 (April 2003): 157–95.

_____. "The Orations of the Vatican II Missal: Policies for Revision." *Communio* 30 (Winter 2003): 621–53.

_____. "The Collects at Sunday Mass: An Examination of the Revisions of Vatican II." *Nova et Vetera* 3/1 (Winter 2005): 5–38.

Ward, A. and C. Johnson, "The Sources of the Roman Missal 1975," *Notitiæ* 22 (1986): 445-747 and 32 (1996): 7-179.

_____. "Fontes liturgici, sources of the Roman Missal: Prefaces." *Notitae* 24 (1987): 507-538.

Other Titles by the Author

1. **Speak O Lord** (On the Word of God in the Liturgy)
2. **Let us Celebrate** (On the Eucharistic Liturgy)
3. *Kairos*: The Sacred Time (On the Liturgical Year and the Liturgy of the Hours)
4. **The Vessel**: A Contemplative Journey with St. Paul (Meditation for Priests & Religious)
5. **Threshold of Love**: Pauline Family Meditation (Meditation based on the Letters of St. Paul and the Rite of Marriage)
6. **Prophet Amos in India** (Drama on Social Justice)
7. **Isail Iraivarthai** (Audio CD-Songs in Tamil based on the prayers in the Bible)
8. **Arulin Uttru** (Audio CD-Songs and skits in Tamil on Sacraments)
9. **Irai Uravil Vazha** (On the Eucharist – Book in Tamil)
10. **Arul Vazhvu** (On the Sacraments – Book in Tamil)
11. **Neengal Ivaru Jebiungal** (Tamil)
12. **Pastoral Visit Guide Book** (Tamil)
13. **Diocesan Pastoral Council**
14. **Diocesan Property Management**
15. **Anburavai Noki** (Diocesan Golden Jubilee Souvenir - Editor - Tamil)
16. **St. Peter's Link** (Jubilee Publication – Editor)
17. **New Missal Same Mass**: Understanding the English Translation of the New Roman Missal
18. **My Beloved**: Theological and Sacramental Reflections on the Christian Priesthood